Praise for *AI-Powered Cataloguing*

'*AI-Powered Cataloguing* is a timely and highly practical resource that bridges the gap between traditional cataloguing and emerging AI-powered workflows across library environments. Hannes Lowagie brings both technical expertise and a deep understanding of bibliographic applications. A must-read for library professionals exploring real-world automation in an AI-driven world.'
Dr Michalis Gerolimos, Deputy Head of Cataloguing, National Library of Greece

'Hannes Lowagie boldly confronts the controversial and often misunderstood field of AI-based bibliographic cataloguing, showcasing the design and real-world outcomes of a pioneering implementation. At a time when much of the discourse remains speculative or abstract, this book delivers much-needed clarity, substance and direction. It not only illuminates technical possibilities but also redefines the evolving role of the cataloguer, urging readers to rethink the profession as a space for reinvention, not replacement.'
Roberto Gómez, Head of Bibliographic Standards Office, National Library of Spain

'As well as being a usefully practical guide to creating an online tool for cataloguing, Hannes' book is an excellent primer for anyone interested in thinking about the future of cataloguing. His comprehensive text invites us all to improve our workflows and update our understanding of the potential for our metadata creation.'
Jenny Wright, Chief Metadata Officer, Bibliographic Data Services

AF794927

AI-Powered Cataloguing

Every purchase of a Facet book helps to fund CILIP's advocacy, awareness and accreditation programmes for information professionals.

AI-Powered Cataloguing

A Practical Guide to Building a Cataloguing Application with Power Apps

Hannes Lowagie

facet publishing

© Hannes Lowagie 2025

Published by Facet Publishing
www.facetpublishing.co.uk

Facet Publishing is wholly owned by CILIP:
the Library and Information Association.

The author has asserted his right under the Copyright, Designs and Patents Act 1988 to be identified as author of this work.

Except as otherwise permitted under the Copyright, Designs and Patents Act 1988 this publication may only be reproduced, stored or transmitted in any form or by any means, with the prior permission of the publisher, or, in the case of reprographic reproduction, in accordance with the terms of a licence issued by The Copyright Licensing Agency. Enquiries concerning reproduction outside those terms should be sent to info@facetpublishing.co.uk.

Every effort has been made to contact the holders of copyright material reproduced in this text, and thanks are due to them for permission to reproduce the material indicated. If there are any queries, please contact the publisher.

Disclaimer
This book is an independent publication and is not an official Microsoft Power Apps product. It is not sponsored, endorsed or paid for by Microsoft. The content is based on the author's personal experience and research, aimed at helping librarians and information professionals integrate AI and automation into cataloguing.

British Library Cataloguing in Publication Data
A catalogue record for this book is available from the British Library.

ISBN 978-1-78330-807-1 (paperback)
ISBN 978-1-78330-808-8 (hardback)
ISBN 978-1-78330-809-5 (PDF)
ISBN 978-1-78330-810-1 (EPUB)

MIX
Paper | Supporting responsible forestry
FSC® C013604

The manufacturer's authorised representative in the EU for product safety is Logos Europe, 9 rue Nicolas Poussin, 17000 La Rochelle, France (contact@logoseurope.eu, www.logoseurope.eu).

Typeset from author's files in 10/13pt Palatino and OpenSans by Flagholme Publishing Services.
Printed and made in Great Britain by CPI Group (UK) Ltd, Croydon, CR0 4YY.

To my dear daughters, Maud and Renée.

May your hearts remain human in an AI-driven world.

Contents

Figures and Tables

Figures

Tables

About the Author

Hannes Lowagie is head of the Bibliographic Information Agency at KBR, the Royal Library of Belgium. His team is responsible for cataloguing books received through legal deposit as well as books purchased and donated.

In this role, he initiated the transition to the RDA (Resource Description and Access) cataloguing standards. This modernisation effort has not only updated the rules governing bibliographic cataloguing but has also ensured that the practices remain aligned with the latest developments. He is also overseeing the publication of the Belgian Bibliography, the national bibliography of Belgium.

Hannes and his team are responsible for the cataloguing of books that have been part of the library's collections for years but remain absent from the online catalogue. These absent works need to be identified and catalogued: this process is known as *retrocataloguing*. Retrocataloguing bridges the gap between the rich historical collections housed in the library and the accessibility required by today's researchers and readers. During this project, the project team conceived the idea of creating an application powered by artificial intelligence (AI) to identify bibliographic records efficiently. To bring this vision to life, they tested several tools to evaluate their capabilities and suitability. Hannes oversaw the development of a custom application using Power Apps, leveraging its versatility to address the specific needs of the project. He further refined and optimised the application later, designing and implementing custom flows and modules to enhance its functionality. This experience provided him with valuable knowledge, insights into best practices and important lessons learned.

Hannes has a background as a historian, earning a PhD in History in 2012. He focused his research on late Medieval Flanders, exploring topics such as suicide and urban correspondence. Through these studies, he developed a lasting appreciation for well-organised and accessible catalogues. He often needed reliable bibliographic tools to find and access key documents. This has strongly shaped his professional approach. This book stands as a testament to his commitment to improving cataloguing practices.

Foreword

It is with great pride and excitement that I introduce this book, which documents the creation of an AI-based cataloguing application. I hope it will serve as a guide for innovation in cultural heritage institutions and inspire you.

The Royal Library of Belgium (KBR) is the national scientific library. It collects all Belgian publications and preserves, manages and studies an extensive cultural and historical heritage consisting of some eight million physical objects and even more digital documents. We provide the public with access to information, facilitate research and offer a broad cultural experience.

In a rapidly changing world where technology brings new possibilities every day, users' needs and practices are constantly evolving. Institutions like ours must also progress. KBR's vision is to contribute to the democratic foundations of an increasingly digital society by providing citizens with reliable and sustainable information. That is why we put the user – and the way they process information – at the centre of our activities, integrating new technologies and automation into our entire operation.

The retrocataloguing project we initiated, along with the development of the AI-based application, fits fully into our strategy. It is a project that demanded creativity, expertise and a bold vision of the future. The main goal was to ensure wide access to our vast collections for scholars, researchers and the wider public by applying cutting-edge technology to enrich and streamline our cataloguing workflows.

The development of the application marked a significant milestone in our journey. It demonstrates the power of AI to revolutionise daily operations and symbolises how technology can be harnessed to support human expertise and achieve previously unimaginable goals. The success of this project has motivated us to continue exploring AI's potential as an ally in enhancing the efficiency, accuracy and reach of our work. We are committed to further incorporate AI into our daily workflows in ways that respect ethical principles, safeguard the integrity of our collections and uphold the trust of the communities we serve.

This book is a testament to what can be achieved when vision meets action. It not only details the technical journey behind the creation of the cataloguing app but also serves as a roadmap for future endeavours. We hope that the work we have done will inspire other institutions and professionals to embark on similar projects and collaborate with us in shaping the future of AI in cultural heritage.

At KBR, we believe that knowledge thrives when shared. This book reflects our commitment to fostering innovation and collaboration and we look forward to seeing its impact ripple across the field.

Congratulations to the author for his achievement and to everyone who contributed to this fantastic project.

May this book be an invitation to discovery, progress, and meaningful partnerships.

Sara Lammens
Director, KBR
The National Library of Belgium

Acknowledgements

I would like to express my gratitude to several individuals and groups who made this journey possible and supported me throughout the development of this application and the creation of this book.

First and foremost, my thanks go to Sara Lammens and Sophie Vandepontseele for granting me the opportunity to work on this application. Your belief in the concept, unwavering support and commitment to its financing have been instrumental in bringing this project to life.

I am deeply grateful to Frederik Bisback, developer at Inetum-Realdolmen, for his insightful advice and guidance, which has greatly shaped my work and strengthened the application.

Special thanks are also due to Jenny Wright, current Chair of the European RDA Interest Group (EURIG), for her kind invitation to London to speak about the application at the Metadata and Discovery Group of CILIP. This opportunity not only allowed me to present my ideas to a wider audience but also led to a valuable introduction to Facet Publishing through her follow-up e-mail correspondence. Your encouragement has been pivotal in this endeavour.

To all the cataloguers at the bibliographic information agency of KBR, I owe a debt of gratitude. Your enthusiastic engagement in testing the application, sharing constructive feedback and identifying key areas for improvement have been invaluable. Your openness to new ideas and your collaborative spirit inspired me to continuously refine and enhance the application. The help of Lennart Vandamme and Julie Van Woensel at the beginning of the project has been especially useful. I thank Tan Lu, a researcher at KBR, for his valuable insights into how AI truly works.

I would like to extend my thanks to my wife, whose support and patience have been my anchor throughout this process. During the evenings when I was engrossed in either the application or this book, your understanding and encouragement gave me the strength to persevere. I also must thank my two wonderful daughters, now aged four and six, who have taught me the importance of balance. Their joyful insistence on playtime and their ability to remind me of life beyond work brought me much-needed breaks and the energy to continue.

To all of you, my sincerest thanks.

Abbreviations

AI	Artificial Intelligence
AACR	Anglo-American Cataloguing Rules
API	Application Programming Interface
BIBFRAME	Bibliographic Framework Initiative
BNE	Biblioteca Nacional de España
COVID-19	Coronavirus Disease
CSV	Comma-separated Values
DDC	Dewey Decimal Classification
DNB	German National Library
FAIR	Findable, Accessible, Interoperable, Reusable
FRBR	Functional Requirements for Bibliographic Records
FTP	File Transfer Protocol
GPT	Generative Pre-training Transformer
GPU	Graphics Processing Units
HTR	Handwritten Text Recognition
IFLA LRM	International Federation of Library Associations and Institutions Library Reference Model
ISBD	International Standard Bibliographic Description
ISBDM	ISBD for Manifestation
ISBN	International Standard Book Number
ISNI	International Standard Name Identifier
ISSN	International Standard Serial Number
JSON	JavaScript Object Notation
KBR	Royal Library of Belgium
LCSH	Library of Congress Subject Headings
LLM	Large Language Model
LMS	Library Management System
LOC	Library of Congress
MARC	Machine-Readable Cataloging
ML	Machine Learning
NLP	Natural Language Processing

OCR	Optical Character Recognition
OPAC	Online Public Access Catalog
RDA	Resource Description and Access
RDF	Resource Description Framework
RSC	RDA Steering Committee
SKOS	Simple Knowledge Organization System
SRU	Search/Retrieve via URL
TSV	Tab-separated Values
UAT	User Acceptance Testing
UDC	Universal Decimal Classification
UI	User Interface
URL	Uniform Resource Locator
URI	Uniform Resource Identifier
WLIC	World Library and Information Congress (IFLA)

Introduction

The year 2020 at KBR, the Royal Library of Belgium, began like any other. We started by reviewing the previous year's statistics, evaluating our progress and outlining plans for the months ahead. Our cataloguers, as always, continued their meticulous work, ensuring that new publications were properly catalogued and integrated into the collection. It was business as usual. At that time, we had all heard murmurs about a novel virus emerging from China. It seemed distant, a topic for news headlines but not something that would impact our day-to-day operations. There was little sense of urgency and certainly no reason to believe that our routines would soon be upended.

That sense of calm quickly changed in March 2020. Almost overnight, the Belgian government took swift and dramatic measures to curb the spread of what was now known as COVID-19. Our Prime Minister announced a nationwide shutdown. All pubs, restaurants and social venues were ordered to close. Public gatherings were banned and life as we knew it came to a sudden halt. The Minister of Health, Maggie De Block, delivered a message that became famous across the country: 'blijf in uw kot' – stay inside your home. This simple yet forceful statement encapsulated the new reality.

For many of us at KBR, this meant a sudden and unexpected shift to remote work. The library's doors were closed and we quickly had to adapt. Each member of the team was assigned tasks that could be completed from home. At first, this transition seemed manageable. The initial weeks of working remotely allowed us to focus on projects that had been on the backburner and we made the best of the situation. However, as the quarantine dragged on, the limitations of working from home began to show, especially as new publications continued to arrive at KBR. The pile of uncatalogued books grew taller. As a result, cataloguers were allowed to return to KBR on a limited basis. Their task was to scan some crucial pages of the books in-house (title and copyright pages and back cover), after which they could return home to finish the bibliographic records. This hybrid approach was a crucial step in maintaining the continuity of our work during the pandemic. Not only did it keep the cataloguing process moving forward, but it also set the foundation for more flexible, adaptive methods that would prove useful long after the pandemic.

Meanwhile, like many other cultural institutions around the world, KBR's reading rooms were initially closed to the public. Access to our vast collections was entirely cut off. Because we recognised the importance of providing timely access to our resources for the researchers and students who depend on them for their work, we took deliberate steps to resume operations. Visitors could return to the reading rooms but for (health) security reasons we asked them to reserve their books online in advance. The lack of a fully digitised catalogue however meant that certain holdings were not as easily discoverable, especially for users without specific titles in mind. Our physical card catalogue, a historically valuable tool, was inaccessible online. In response, we acted swiftly to adapt, exploring innovative solutions to better integrate our digital and physical collections, ensuring that access to our collections remained as seamless as possible. Recognising the modern reality that 'if it is not online, it does not exist for the user', we improved our online data services. One key development was the improvement of our Online Public Access Catalog (OPAC) through the integration of a discovery tool, allowing readers to perform a single search that included both our physical collections and the contents of our electronic resources. Additionally, we implemented an authentication protocol that extended access to previously *intra muros* materials, enabling all authorised users to access these resources remotely with a KBR login and registration. These advancements ensured that our library met the immediate challenges of the pandemic and positioned itself for a more connected and user-friendly future.

Retrocataloguing at KBR

It was at this point that KBR revived the retrocataloguing project, with the aim of addressing the gaps in our catalogue. Our goal was to ensure that every item in our collection was made accessible to researchers and the public through our online catalogue. However, we had several options to consider in how to best approach this monumental task.

The first option was to scan the paper library cards from our physical card catalogue, which held records for many of the older items in our collection. A large portion of this printed catalogue had already been scanned and converted into digital bibliographic records in the early 2000s as part of a previous retrocataloguing effort. However, this approach came with several challenges. One of the primary issues was that some were already treated, others were not well structured or even handwritten, increasing the likelihood of errors and misinterpretation.

As we debated the best path forward, we began to see additional advantages in taking a different approach: working directly with the physical books themselves. By doing this, we could combine the retrocataloguing project with a broader stack inspection. This method would allow us to handle each book, verify its condition and ensure that it was correctly catalogued from the ground up. Rather than relying on the outdated card catalogue, we could focus on the original document itself. This raised another important question: how could we quickly create accurate bibliographic records for so many books? Cataloguing is a time-intensive process and we needed an efficient solution that could handle the scale of the task before us.

To address this, we examined the books in the contemporary collection, particularly those published in the 20th century. Upon closer inspection, we noticed that the title pages of these books contained a wealth of information. Unlike many modern publications where title pages are often minimalist, the title pages of books from that period were rich with details. They included essential bibliographic information such as title, subtitles, mentions of responsibility (authors, translators, editors), the place and name of the publisher, the year of publication and even edition statements – enough information to quickly identify a resource. Recognising the potential of this resource, we came up with an innovative solution: we decided to develop a tool that could read and extract all the relevant information from a book's title page. This tool would need to go beyond simple text recognition. It had to be intelligent enough to detect and differentiate between key bibliographic fields, such as the main title, subtitle, authorship details, publication location, publisher's name, publication year and edition statement.

The first step in our journey was to determine whether there was already a tool available on the market that could meet our needs. After conducting a thorough search, we quickly realised that no such tool existed that could perform this task with the level of precision we required. This discovery led us to explore other options and we turned our attention to the potential of artificial intelligence (AI). It was early 2022 and although the capabilities of AI were already well known in many fields, the specific applications of AI for tasks like ours were still largely unexplored. While AI had been successfully implemented in areas such as image recognition, natural language processing and automation, its use in libraries for tasks like our retrocataloguing project was still in its infancy. At this point, OpenAI had not yet launched its large language model ChatGPT, so there was still a degree of uncertainty — both in the industry and within our own team — about what AI could realistically achieve.

Despite this, we knew that the rapid pace of technological development meant that AI was worth exploring. Automated metadata detection had already been tested and refined for many years. See, for example, Wilhelmina Randtke's article (2013), which discusses the possibilities and pitfalls of automated metadata creation in detail. In Randtke's work, a database of over 30,000 pages from a loose-leaf resource was indexed using digitisation, optical character recognition (OCR) and computer scripts to extract metadata. Where the computer was unable to assign metadata accurately, human review filled the gaps. The study found comparable error rates between automated and human indexing while emphasising the significant time efficiency of automated processes. This illustrates the broader potential of automated metadata creation, particularly in scenarios where large volumes of uniform or semi-uniform documents need to be processed. By integrating automation with human supervision, systems can achieve a balance between efficiency and accuracy. As we considered the applications of AI in this domain, the lessons from projects like Randtke's reminded us of the importance of aligning technological solutions with human input. The idea of using AI to analyse title pages, recognise key bibliographic elements and transform that information into structured records seemed promising. However, there were still many unknowns: Could AI handle the complex nuances of bibliographic data? Would it be able to distinguish between different types of information? And, perhaps most importantly, could it do this accurately and efficiently enough to justify the investment of time and resources?

These were the questions we faced as we began to delve deeper into the possibilities of AI and machine learning. It was clear that while the technology had significant potential, there was still a considerable gap between theoretical possibilities and practical applications for a project like ours. Nonetheless, we remained optimistic, recognising that AI was evolving rapidly and had the potential to revolutionise how we approached not just retrocataloguing but library science as a whole.

We soon discovered that several tools on the market were designed to extract information from structured documents, such as identity cards or invoices. These tools were adept at recognising standard fields like names, addresses, lists of goods or services, prices per unit, total amounts, VAT details and other predefined information. However, while these tools were highly effective for such specific, structured documents, we needed something that could handle the more varied and nuanced data found on the title pages of books.

Some of the available tools offered a useful feature: the ability to test 'custom models'. This feature allowed users to train the tool to recognise and process information from document types that had not been addressed by the pre-existing, built-in models. Essentially, we could customise the tool to work with our unique type of documents. The testing phase for these custom models was often offered for free, providing an excellent opportunity to experiment without committing to a paid service.

During the testing phase, we were able to upload a set of documents – typically anywhere from five to fifty images, depending on the tool – to train the model. We carefully annotated the data fields on each document, marking the information we wanted the AI to recognise, such as titles, authors, subtitles, publication years and publishers. These annotations served as the groundwork for the tool to learn how to identify similar data on unprocessed documents.

After training the model with a small sample of title pages, we were pleased to find that the results were consistently promising. Once the model had been trained, it was capable of accurately detecting the main bibliographic fields from previously unseen scans of title pages. This included essential details such as the title, author and publication information – exactly what we needed to streamline the cataloguing process.

The success of these tests confirmed that, with the right customisation, existing AI tools could be adapted to meet our specific needs. This discovery opened up new possibilities for automating the retrocataloguing project and greatly improved our confidence in the role AI could play in making our collections more accessible.

With our confidence in the potential of AI solidified, we shifted our focus to evaluating other important factors in order to select the best option for moving forward. We needed a solution that would harness the power of AI effectively and offer a user-friendly application capable of visualising detected metadata, allowing for easy validation and modification and seamlessly integrating with our existing IT infrastructure. A key requirement was the ability to embed AI capabilities into a functional application that could operate within an efficient workflow, ensuring that AI-driven processes fit smoothly into our day-to-day operations.

Cost considerations were also a crucial factor in our decision-making process as we aimed to find a solution that provided advanced capabilities without exceeding budget constraints. With all of these factors in mind, we recognised significant potential in the Microsoft Power Platform (www.microsoft.com/en-gb/power-platform) and its suite of tools, including Power Automate, Power Apps and Power BI. This platform offered a comprehensive, adaptable solution that met our technical requirements, while also being cost-effective and capable of supporting our long-term goals for streamlined, AI-enhanced workflows. The Power Platform stood out due to its flexibility and wide range of possibilities. We saw significant potential in using it to develop an application that could meet all our specific requirements – from automating the metadata extraction process to providing a streamlined interface for users to review and edit the data.

Convinced of its potential, we decided to take the next step by contacting a private firm that specialised in Power Platform development. We arranged discussions with their team, clearly outlining our goals and explaining the functionality we needed from the application. We emphasised the importance of creating a system that would automate the cataloguing process and make it simple for users to interact with, verify and refine the data as needed.

After thoroughly communicating our vision, we engaged the firm to develop the custom application we had envisioned. This collaboration was key in bringing together our expertise in library science and their technical know-how, ensuring that the final product would perfectly align with our operational needs.

The aim of this book

Following the completion of this project, I gained a deep understanding of how to develop tools and implement automation processes in the Microsoft Power Platform. Armed with this knowledge, I went on to create my own automated system that generates a bibliographic record by scanning just two to three pages of a book.

I had the opportunity to present this workflow at the World Library and Information Congress (WLIC) 2023 in Rotterdam (Lowagie, 2023a) as well as at several other events afterwards. Each time I shared this innovation, I received the same enthusiastic response, particularly from librarians who recognised the significant potential of the application and from institutions facing the challenge of large, uncatalogued collections.

This widespread interest made me realise how valuable it would be to share the insights I have gained. That is the purpose of this book. It aims to provide a comprehensive guide on how you can create your own automated application or workflow, tailored to meet the specific needs of your institution or collection. Whether you are dealing with a backlog of uncatalogued items or looking to streamline your cataloguing, the book will walk you through the steps to develop a solution that fits your unique requirements. In the end, we will discover that the proposed solution addresses the initial problem but also provides an opportunity to offer users more in-depth information. By transforming text into structured data, the solution enables the presentation of archival or library documents in a new, more accessible format. This shift can enhance the user experience by allowing them to interact with and explore the content in ways that go beyond traditional reading. For example, documents can be analysed, queried and even integrated with other data sources, offering users a richer, more engaging way to access information. In this way, the solution does not just store or display documents — it turns them into a dynamic resource, making them more useful and informative, especially in the field of Digital Humanities.

This book aims to transform the way we approach cataloguing. Combining innovation with practicality, it provides a step-by-step guide to creating automated workflows and applications tailored to library and archival needs. By bridging traditional cataloguing methods with modern, AI-driven solutions, this resource empowers readers to address challenges such as uncatalogued collections and the demand for more accessible, enriched metadata.

In this book, we will focus on Microsoft's Power Platform, an innovative suite of tools designed to simplify and enhance the development of applications, automate workflows, analyse data and create virtual agents. Rather than providing a comprehensive overview of every (AI-)tool and application available in the technology landscape, we will concentrate on the Power Platform specifically. The technology world is constantly evolving, with new tools and features emerging all the time and attempting to cover everything would inevitably result in missing some tools or details. Instead, my aim is to offer a deep dive into the Power Platform, an area I know well and where nearly any cataloguing or technical challenge can be effectively addressed. My confidence in the Power Platform stems from its unique combination of flexibility, user-friendly design and powerful integration capabilities. It also allows users to connect with a vast array of external platforms and services, enabling solutions that can seamlessly interact with other technologies to meet diverse needs.

One of the most significant challenges librarians face when considering the adoption of AI technology is the associated cost. Research has revealed that implementing AI in libraries often necessitates a significant financial investment, creating a substantial barrier, particularly for institutions operating under constrained budgets during this period of transformation. For example, Tella, Odunola and Lawal (2023) highlighted that limited funding is among the most critical challenges faced by cataloguing and classification librarians in adopting AI technologies in Nigerian academic libraries. Their findings underscore the lack of strategic plans for AI implementation, exacerbating these financial constraints. Similarly, Koresi (2024) has pointed out that AI adoption requires considerable financial resources, which many libraries are unable to afford amid ongoing changes. While it is true that platforms like Microsoft Power Platform are not free and AI functionalities are considered premium features, this tool provides a cost-effective solution. Although there is a licensing fee involved (an overview of this will be provided later), obtaining a premium account grants full access to AI services without any additional costs. This makes it an affordable option for libraries that are ready to embrace innovation but need to do so in a budget-conscious manner. By offering a balance between cost and functionality, the Power Platform opens the door for libraries to harness AI without the need for excessive financial resources, enabling them to keep pace with technological advancements.

The journey begins in Chapter 1, which lays the foundation by exploring the fundamentals of cataloguing and metadata. It examines the evolution from traditional to modern approaches and highlights the importance of inclusivity in bibliographic records. This chapter provides the essential context to understand how automation and AI can complement and enhance existing practices.

Chapter 2 introduces the Microsoft Power Platform, delving into its ecosystem of tools: Power Apps, Power Automate and AI Builder. Readers will find practical guidance on licensing and setup, ensuring they are equipped to navigate the platform effectively. This chapter sets the stage for understanding how these tools can streamline workflows and improve cataloguing efficiency.

The focus on artificial intelligence takes centre stage in Chapter 3, where readers will learn to integrate AI into their workflows. Detailed, step-by-step instructions demonstrate how to use Microsoft AI Builder to train models, extract key information and generate inclusive metadata. This chapter illustrates how AI can transform raw text into structured data, offering new ways to interact with and analyse collections.

In Chapter 4, the book takes a hands-on approach, guiding readers through the process of building a customised cataloguing application within the Power Platform. From app design to automation and implementation, this chapter equips readers with the tools and strategies to create practical solutions tailored to their unique needs.

Finally, Chapter 5 addresses the deployment and maintenance of the application, focusing on critical aspects such as data security, troubleshooting and user training. It also explores the broader potential of the Power Platform across GLAM (Galleries, Libraries, Archives and Museums) institutions, showcasing how these tools can manage diverse collections and expand cataloguing possibilities.

By the conclusion, readers will have gained the knowledge and confidence to develop cost-effective, innovative solutions using the Power Platform. Whether improving efficiency, enhancing metadata accessibility or reimagining cataloguing practices, this book offers a roadmap to harnessing technology for a more dynamic and inclusive future in information management.

CHAPTER 1

Cataloguing Today and in the Future

Introduction to cataloguing and metadata

What is cataloguing and why does it matter in libraries?

Cataloguing is the structured process of creating both bibliographic and authority records to represent the materials within a library's collection. These records are crucial for organising, identifying and facilitating access to library resources. Each cataloguing record includes essential data such as the title of the work, the author or creator, publication details (like the place, publisher and year) and relevant subjects or classifications. This information is meticulously compiled and then entered into a catalogue, which serves as the foundation for resource discovery within the library.

The primary purpose of cataloguing is to help users find, identify, select and obtain library resources. In the modern library environment, catalogues are typically made accessible online through an OPAC. This online platform enables users to search for and locate specific materials, whether they are books, journal articles or digital media, by using various search criteria such as keywords, author names, titles or subjects. By organising materials in this way, cataloguing ensures that a vast array of information is accessible in a clear and manageable format, making it easier for patrons to explore and retrieve the resources they need. By putting data into a catalogue and making that catalogue accessible online, libraries can ensure that their collections are easily searchable and discoverable by users, allowing for a smooth and efficient resource discovery process. A well-organised catalogue provides users with detailed information that allows them to locate specific items, even in vast collections. Whether a user is searching for a particular book, a journal article or a piece of audiovisual material, the catalogue functions as a roadmap, guiding them to the exact resource they need. Cataloguing plays a critical role in information retrieval, enabling both simple and advanced searches. By offering bibliographic details and subject-based classifications, cataloguing helps users explore related materials and uncover resources they may not have initially known about, enhancing the research and learning process.

Cataloguing supports individual users in finding specific materials. It allows libraries to manage large collections systematically and maintain consistency in how materials are classified and retrieved. Without cataloguing, library collections would become disorganised and virtually inaccessible. Furthermore, in national and university libraries, which manage vast and diverse collections, cataloguing holds particular significance. These institutions often house extensive collections that include rare, historical and culturally significant works. Accurate and comprehensive cataloguing in these settings helps to preserve this cultural heritage, ensuring that valuable materials are not lost to obscurity but instead are made available for research, study and public access on a global scale, promoting scholarly research and cross-cultural understanding. In other words, through cataloguing, libraries serve their immediate communities and contribute to the broader academic and cultural landscape. In this context, cataloguing is more than a technical task — it is a vital process that ensures knowledge is systematically preserved, discoverable and shared with the world.

Metadata's broader impact

Metadata, often described as 'data about data', is the foundational information created during the cataloguing process that plays a critical role in organising, describing and facilitating the retrieval of resources in libraries. In simple terms, metadata provides the structured information necessary to make library materials findable and accessible, serving as the key to unlocking the contents of a collection. There are several types of metadata used in libraries, each serving a distinct purpose:

1 Descriptive metadata: This type of metadata provides information that helps to identify and describe a resource. It includes elements such as the title, author, publisher, publication date and subjects. This is the most familiar form of metadata as it is directly linked to how users search for and find materials in a catalogue. Descriptive metadata can also include information about how different components of a resource are related to each other or how they are related to an authority record.
2 Administrative metadata: This category encompasses the behind-the-scenes details that help manage and preserve a resource. It includes information such as file format, copyright data, access restrictions and information on how a resource was created or digitised. For digital

collections, administrative metadata can also include technical details like file size, digitisation method and storage location.

Descriptive metadata was primarily used to describe physical resources. However, in the age of digital collections, its role has expanded significantly. Digital metadata is essential for ensuring the discoverability of resources across large databases and for integrating digital and physical collections. Whether it is a physical book on a shelf or a digital document stored in an online repository, the metadata allows users to find what they are looking for quickly and efficiently. It also facilitates interoperability, ensuring that different systems and databases can communicate with each other, making it possible for users to search across multiple platforms.

While metadata is crucial for helping individual patrons locate specific resources, its value extends far beyond resource discovery. Increasingly, metadata itself has become a rich dataset for researchers in various fields. Scholars use metadata to study patterns in publishing, authorship and cultural trends, as well as to conduct bibliometric and bibliographic analyses.

For example, in translation studies, projects like BELTRANS at the Royal Library of Belgium (KBR) rely heavily on metadata to trace the history and evolution of literary translations over time. By examining metadata about translations, researchers can uncover which works were translated, by whom and how often, revealing important insights into cultural exchange and literary influence. Similarly, in cultural and historical studies, library descriptive metadata can provide a wealth of information about societal trends. Researchers can analyse metadata across time periods to study the impact of certain authors or publishers, the proliferation of particular genres or the dissemination of knowledge across geographic regions.

One of the key objectives of modern cataloguing is to ensure that data is accessible and usable in a wide variety of contexts. This is where the concept of FAIR principles comes in: catalogue data should be Findable, Accessible, Interoperable and Reusable. By adhering to these principles, libraries ensure that their data can be easily discovered and accessed by users, not just within the library's own catalogue but also through external systems and networks. FAIR metadata is easily discoverable, can be accessed by anyone regardless of location, integrates smoothly with other data systems and is flexible enough to be reused in various research and analytical projects.

One important step toward making metadata FAIR is publishing it as linked open data. Linked open data is structured data that is interconnected across multiple datasets and is openly available for use by anyone. For libraries, publishing their catalogue data as linked open data allows their resources to be part of a larger global knowledge network. This means that researchers, scholars and even other libraries can cross-reference materials from multiple institutions, facilitating more in-depth, interconnected research. By ensuring that metadata is published as linked open data, libraries increase the visibility of their collections and contribute to a larger, more accessible web of knowledge. For example, a library's bibliographic data, when made available as linked open data, can be used by researchers worldwide to trace the dissemination of ideas, compare publishing trends or study the development of certain fields of knowledge.

In conclusion, metadata plays a central role in both the day-to-day functioning of libraries and in the broader landscape of academic and cultural research. While it serves the practical purpose of helping patrons find and access materials, it also serves as a powerful dataset for understanding larger trends in literature, publishing and culture.

Key elements of cataloguing records

The International Standard Bibliographic Description (ISBD) has played a fundamental role in library cataloguing since its inception in the 1970s, providing a framework for creating standardised bibliographic records. Designed by the International Federation of Library Associations and Institutions (IFLA), ISBD aimed to ensure consistency and comprehensiveness in cataloguing across different languages and countries. It specified a set of elements required to describe a resource thoroughly, such as title, author, edition and publication details, which have become essential for effective resource discovery and library management.

Although ISBD laid the groundwork for modern cataloguing practices, the field has evolved significantly. The Anglo-American Cataloguing Rules (AACR) were a critical development in this evolution. First published in 1967 (edited by C. Sumner Spalding), AACR incorporated ISBD principles and adapted them for use in English-speaking libraries. The AACR underwent multiple revisions, culminating in the AACR2, which further refined bibliographic description practices (1978, edited by Michael Gorman and Paul W. Winkler). There were initial plans to revise AACR2 and develop a new third edition known as AACR3. However, in 2005, these plans were abandoned. The reason was clear: the world of information had undergone a significant transformation. The rise of the internet, the emergence of the semantic web (RDF) and the proliferation of electronic publications meant that a simple revision of the existing rules would no longer suffice.

The cataloguing community recognised that a more radical approach was necessary to keep pace with these changes. This realisation led to the decision to create a completely new standard, which resulted in the development of

Resource Description and Access (RDA). RDA was designed to address the complexities and challenges of cataloguing in a digital and interconnected world. It aimed to provide a flexible, comprehensive framework that could accommodate both traditional resources and the diverse formats emerging in the digital age. Unlike its predecessors, RDA was not just a set of rules; it represented a shift towards a more user-focused, adaptable and inclusive standard that could support the evolving needs of libraries and their users, aligning with the principles of the Functional Requirements for Bibliographic Records (FRBR) and later the IFLA Library Reference Model (IFLA LRM), to better represent relationships between resources. This new standard marked a significant departure from the past, setting the stage for a more integrated approach to resource description, one that could fully embrace the dynamic nature of information in the 21st century.

As cataloguing evolves, ISBD and RDA work together to offer a more adaptable system for bibliographic description, accommodating both traditional print resources and modern digital formats. ISBD for Manifestation (ISBDM) is a specialised implementation of the IFLA LRM that focuses solely on the Manifestation entity. It offers detailed stipulations and guidance for describing a single manifestation, its relationships to other manifestations and its connections to other LRM entities. This design aligns well with RDA, which also adheres to an entity-based cataloguing model grounded in the WEMI (Work, Expression, Manifestation and Item) structure. While ISBDM primarily addresses the Manifestation level, it can complement RDA's broader framework by providing a more granular and standardised approach to manifestation-level metadata. In practical terms, ISBDM can enhance RDA's capabilities by offering more detailed, standardised metadata for manifestations, which is crucial for interoperability in linked open data and relational database environments. The flexibility of ISBDM to function as a standalone tool or alongside other IFLA LRM implementations allows it to be integrated into RDA workflows. This integration would enable cataloguers to use ISBDM for precise manifestation descriptions while leveraging RDA for a holistic view of the bibliographic resource, encompassing all WEMI entities.

Moreover, ISBDM's online optimisation and structured navigation support the dynamic and flexible metadata creation processes that RDA promotes, making it easier to incorporate into existing cataloguing systems. The shared emphasis on structured, entity-based metadata and interoperability means that ISBDM and RDA can work together to provide comprehensive, nuanced descriptions of bibliographic resources, supporting more accurate resource discovery and data sharing across different platforms and systems. This ongoing evolution is crucial for enhancing the accuracy and accessibility of library collections in a rapidly changing information landscape.

In the IFLA LRM, the overall model of RDA and ISBDM, the Item is the only physical entity within the WEMI model. It represents the tangible embodiment of a resource, such as a particular book or a specific digital file. From this physical Item, we can extract valuable metadata that corresponds to different levels of the WEMI hierarchy, including the Manifestation, Expression and Work.

Starting with the Manifestation, which reflects the publication details of the resource, key elements we can detect from the Item include the place of publication, the name of the publisher, the date of publication, the title proper and any additional title information like subtitles or parallel titles. Certain author roles, such as those of the translator or illustrator, are specifically associated with the Manifestation level of the bibliographic record. These roles are directly linked to the particular edition or version of a work as it has been published or presented. For example, a translator contributes to a specific translation of a text, while an illustrator's work is tied to a particular edition that features their illustrations. This makes their contributions unique to that manifestation, distinguishing it from other versions of the same work.

In addition to author roles, various identifiers and physical attributes are key elements that define a manifestation. For example, the International Standard Book Number (ISBN) serves as a unique identifier for a specific edition, allowing it to be distinguished from all other editions. Similarly, the extent, which refers to the number of pages or duration of a resource and dimensions and describes its physical size, are essential for accurately describing the manifestation. All these elements are vital for precisely identifying and describing the specific version of a resource that the Item represents. They provide detailed information that differentiates one manifestation from another and enhances the resource's discoverability and accessibility. By accurately capturing these attributes, cataloguers ensure that users can easily find the exact edition or version they need, whether they are searching for a particular translation, a specific illustrated edition or a unique format of the work. This level of detail is crucial for effective resource management and user satisfaction in library and information systems.

As we move up the bibliographic hierarchy, the Expression level captures details about the intellectual or artistic realisation of a Work. This level provides critical information that helps to distinguish different versions or manifestations of the same fundamental content. It encompasses attributes such as the language or the content type. For example, at the Expression level, we identify whether the resource is a textual document, a musical score or a visual material like an illustrated book or artwork. This categorisation is crucial because it conveys how the content is structured and presented to the user. The Expression level also specifies the language in which the resource is expressed, differentiating between, say, an English translation and a French translation of the same work. Understanding these details at the Expression level is essential because they provide context about how the Work has been interpreted, adapted or translated. It helps cataloguers and users alike to grasp the nuances of the resource. By capturing these attributes, the Expression level enriches the bibliographic record, supporting a more nuanced and comprehensive understanding of the resource's content and format. This deeper insight is invaluable for researchers, librarians and users seeking specific versions or adaptations of a work.

At the Work level, we focus on the broader conceptual essence of a resource, which remains consistent regardless of its physical form or presentation. This is where we identify the original title of the Work and the primary author or creator, capturing the core intellectual or artistic content that underlies all its variations. The Work level represents the foundational ideas or themes that are expressed through different translations, adaptations, editions and formats. By understanding this level, we can link various Expressions and Manifestations back to a single, unified Work.

By analysing the physical Item, we can gather a comprehensive set of metadata that encompasses all three levels of the bibliographic hierarchy: Manifestation, Expression and Work. This process allows us to construct a detailed and structured description of the resource, capturing not only its physical characteristics and specific presentation details but also its intellectual content and conceptual origins. Such an approach is invaluable for accurate cataloguing as it ensures that every aspect of the resource is thoroughly documented and organised. This description significantly enhances the discoverability and accessibility of library collections. Users can more easily locate the specific version or edition they need, while also understanding how different versions relate to the original Work. For example, someone searching for a translated edition of a novel will be able to see all available translations and their respective details, providing a clear view of how each relates to the original text. In Chapter 3, we will delve into which elements can be detected through AI and how. This will include a discussion on the potential of AI to recognise and extract metadata across all three levels, ultimately supporting more efficient and precise resource management.

In addition, certain fields play a crucial role in supporting both user searches and effective resource management. For example, subject headings and classification systems help users discover materials that are relevant to their interests by categorising resources according to their topics. Libraries typically rely on controlled vocabularies, such as the Library of Congress Subject Headings (LCSH), to ensure that the categorisation is consistent and standardised across their collections. This makes it easier for users to find all the materials related to a specific subject, regardless of the resource's format or title variations.

The call number, on the other hand, is an essential element for locating a specific resource within the physical space of the library. It acts as a unique identifier that indicates its precise position on the shelves. This system serves as a vital link between the library catalogue, which lists all available resources and the physical collection, guiding users directly to the book or item they are looking for.

The accuracy and consistency of these cataloguing elements are crucial for efficient library operations. Precise metadata improves resource discovery, ensuring users can easily locate the materials they need. Accuracy also facilitates interlibrary cooperation. Many libraries participate in shared cataloguing initiatives or interlibrary loan systems, where they borrow or share resources with other institutions. Consistent use of metadata and cataloguing standards ensures that records are understandable and usable across different libraries and systems.

Controlled vocabularies, such as the LCSH mentioned earlier, are essential tools in the world of cataloguing for maintaining consistency and clarity in bibliographic records. They ensure that subjects, names and other descriptive elements are represented in a standardised manner, which helps avoid confusion and ambiguity. For example, authority control — the process of establishing and maintaining consistent forms for personal names, corporate bodies and subjects — is critical to ensuring that all works by a particular author are correctly attributed to the same individual, rather than being mistakenly linked to another person with a similar or identical name. In this context, international identifiers like the International Standard Name Identifier (ISNI) play a pivotal role. ISNI provides a unique identifier for individuals and organisations involved in the creation, production and distribution of content. By assigning a distinct numerical code to each entity, ISNI helps disambiguate authors, performers and corporate bodies that may otherwise be confused due to shared or similar names. This is particularly important in large-scale catalogues where multiple creators with the same or similar names are common.

Using these controlled vocabularies and authority control mechanisms ensures that library records are precise and reliable. It allows users to easily find all works associated with a specific author, corporate body or subject, without the risk of encountering irrelevant or misleading results. This level of precision is crucial for research and scholarship as it enables users to navigate complex bibliographic information efficiently and accurately. Furthermore, it supports the interoperability of data across different library systems, enabling better resource sharing and more effective management of library collections worldwide.

Overview of cataloguing standards

To ensure that cataloguing records are usable and consistent across libraries and digital systems, cataloguing practices follow established standards. These standards are essential for maintaining the accuracy of bibliographic records, enhancing interoperability between systems and ensuring that users can find materials across different platforms. The most widely used standard for encoding bibliographic and authority records in a format that computers can read is Machine-Readable Cataloging (MARC). It was developed in the 1960s and has since become the foundation of library catalogues worldwide. MARC records are structured into data fields and subfields (indicated with a $ (e.g., 245$a for Main Title)), making it easy for library management systems to store, retrieve and display catalogue data. The number of the data field or the character for the subfield is defined by the type of marc. Most used are UNIMARC and MARC 21. In KBR, we have catalogued in MARC21 since 2018.

While MARC remains effective for many cataloguing purposes, its rigid structure and limited ability to represent linked data have led to the development of newer standards. That is why the Library of Congress developed BIBFRAME (Bibliographic Framework Initiative). BIBFRAME is a modern alternative to MARC, designed to support linked open data and improve the ability of library catalogues to connect with other datasets on the web. BIBFRAME uses RDF (Resource Description Framework), a standard for encoding metadata in a way that links data across systems. This allows libraries to publish their catalogue data as linked open data, making it more discoverable and reusable by other institutions and researchers. By embracing BIBFRAME, libraries can integrate their resources more effectively into the broader web of knowledge, allowing for more sophisticated data relationships and connections between various cultural, academic and archival resources.

BIBFRAME and MARC provide the framework for organising where specific fields should be placed within cataloguing records, while the cataloguing guidelines dictate how these fields are filled in. At KBR, we are gradually updating our cataloguing rules and practices to align with the above-mentioned RDA standards. Unlike previous cataloguing standards, RDA is designed to be more flexible and comprehensive, providing detailed guidance for cataloguing a wide range of resources. By adopting RDA, we aim to improve the consistency and accessibility of our catalogue, ensuring that users can easily find and retrieve information across different types of resources. This transition reflects our commitment to staying up to date with evolving library standards and enhancing the quality of our bibliographic records.

RDA includes a data model and the RDA Registry, which provides a linked data and Semantic Web representation of entities, elements and terminologies approved by the RDA Steering Committee (RSC). You can find this registry at www.rdaregistry.info. This allows for better integration of catalogue data with the wider web of linked data, enhancing interoperability and global resource sharing.

Interoperability and data sharing

One of the main objectives of cataloguing standards like MARC, BIBFRAME and RDA is to promote interoperability. Interoperability refers to the ability of catalogue data to be understood, exchanged and used across various library systems, platforms and institutions, regardless of geographic location or software differences. This means that a record created by one library can be seamlessly interpreted and used by another, even if they are on opposite sides of the world or using entirely different cataloguing software.

The importance of interoperability therefore extends beyond just record sharing within individual libraries. It plays a pivotal role in facilitating broader data sharing, allowing libraries to contribute their catalogue records to larger, shared databases, such as WorldCat or other union catalogues. For example, in Belgium, the national union catalogue, UNICAT, serves as a collective resource for Belgian libraries (national library, university library and libraries from heritage institutions). These union catalogues enable users to search for materials across multiple libraries simultaneously, increasing access to a vast array of resources that might otherwise be unavailable at their home institution.

Interoperability also supports critical services like interlibrary loans, where users can request materials from other libraries when their own does not have the desired items. This enhances resource availability and fosters collaboration between libraries, ultimately improving the overall user experience by ensuring that information and materials are more readily accessible on a global scale.

The role of inclusivity in cataloguing

The importance of inclusivity in bibliographic records

As the world evolves, so does our approach to cataloguing. With each passing day, we acquire more knowledge and, as a result, users' information needs grow, diversify and shift in exciting ways. New genres emerge, reflecting the broadening scope of creative expression and academic inquiry. Languages and cultural contexts intermingle within individual countries more than ever before, creating a demand for catalogues that are linguistically diverse and culturally inclusive. These changes mean that cataloguing can't remain static; it must adapt and expand to meet the needs of a constantly changing world. Cataloguing has to embrace flexibility and innovation, evolving to capture not just the latest knowledge but also the values and diverse identities of today's users. This ongoing transformation is essential for keeping catalogues relevant, accessible and truly reflective of our complex, interconnected world.

Inclusivity in cataloguing is essential for ensuring that libraries accurately reflect the diverse voices, experiences and cultures that shape our world. Libraries serve as gatekeepers of knowledge, preserving and providing access to information across a wide range of subjects, disciplines and perspectives. However, traditional cataloguing practices have often prioritised Western, Eurocentric and male-dominated viewpoints, unintentionally marginalising or overlooking the contributions of other communities, particularly those from non-Western, Indigenous, LGBTQ+ and minority groups. This lack of representation in bibliographic records can lead to significant gaps in the discoverability and accessibility of diverse materials, limiting the breadth of knowledge available to users. This issue has recently been addressed in *Inclusive Cataloguing: Histories, Contexts, and Reparative Approaches* (Billey, Nelson and Uhl, 2024).

Inclusivity in cataloguing is not just about adding more books to a collection – it is about ensuring that the materials are described in a way that acknowledges and respects their cultural, historical and social contexts. When catalogue records use biased or outdated terms or when they fail to capture the richness of a work's perspective, it diminishes the ability of users to fully engage with and understand these resources. Furthermore, cataloguing inclusivity impacts how scholars, students and the general public can conduct research as it directly affects their ability to find relevant materials that reflect a broad range of voices.

One of the most notable challenges has been the use of outdated or even offensive terminology in subject headings. Older cataloguing systems often reflected the language and perspectives of their time, leading to the use of derogatory or culturally insensitive terms to describe certain groups. For example, subject headings might have labelled communities based on stereotypes or colonial viewpoints, reinforcing harmful narratives instead of accurately representing the diversity of experiences and identities within those communities.

This topic requires special attention because cataloguing inclusivity is not currently an automatic process. It demands conscious, deliberate efforts to recognise and correct the biases embedded in existing cataloguing systems. However, by automating parts of the cataloguing process, particularly through the use of AI, we can significantly improve inclusivity.

AI's potential role in promoting inclusivity

As libraries evolve and technology becomes more integrated into cataloguing workflows, addressing the historical shortcomings of traditional systems becomes even more critical. Automating these tasks with AI can help identify and reduce bias, ensuring more equitable and representative bibliographic records. Inclusivity in cataloguing will ensure that all voices are heard, all stories are told and that future generations have access to a richer, more accurate representation of the world's knowledge. To achieve inclusivity in cataloguing through automation, it is essential to use an inclusive vocabulary for classification, ensuring that subject headings and keywords reflect diverse perspectives and modern, respectful language. AI can assist by suggesting more inclusive alternatives, but this relies heavily on how the training set is created. A non-biased training set is key and it should include a wide range of materials from various cultures, languages and perspectives. By feeding AI models with data that accurately represents marginalised voices and non-Western materials, the system can learn to categorise resources in a way that reflects the diversity of human experience, avoiding the replication of past biases. Recently, Europeana published a vocabulary that can help identify potential bias. It is the result of the DE-BIAS project about detecting and curating harmful language (https://pro.europeana.eu/page/the-de-bias-vocabulary). This approach fosters a more equitable cataloguing process, where both language and structure work together to ensure fair representation.

AI has the potential to help libraries detect and reduce biases in how records are created. AI can help librarians use more inclusive and modern language in cataloguing. By processing texts and subject headings, AI can suggest terms and keywords that reflect the evolving language around marginalised groups. If your training set is trained using more sensitive, updated terms for racial and ethnic groups, only those terms will be suggested.

That is why – and we will talk about subject indexing later in this book – the classification model needs to be trained on diverse datasets to avoid perpetuating existing biases. This means incorporating works from non-Western contexts, LGBTQ+ voices and other marginalised groups into the training data, ensuring AI systems are culturally aware and sensitive in their output. One of the key challenges in using AI for inclusivity in cataloguing is the risk of bias in the training data. If AI models are trained on datasets that reflect traditional or biased cataloguing practices, they may simply replicate those biases. Libraries need to invest in curating diverse and representative training sets. That is an error we made early in the process. We created a training set based on the existing summaries and linked subject terms from our own catalogue as well as from external sources. However, we quickly discovered that these datasets contained numerous errors and inherent biases. For example, certain subjects were underrepresented and outdated or even offensive terms were used in place of more inclusive language. This was a clear reminder that relying solely on traditional cataloguing practices to build AI training sets can perpetuate the very biases we aim to eliminate. It became evident that to truly harness AI for inclusivity, we need to critically assess and refine the training data itself, ensuring it aligns with modern values of equity and representation. Without this step, AI will only reinforce the historical limitations of cataloguing systems rather than challenge and improve them.

While AI can play a valuable role in enhancing inclusivity in cataloguing, human input and oversight remains crucial. Librarians must carefully assess AI-generated metadata to ensure it meets ethical and inclusive standards. For example, even when AI suggests terms, it is the cataloguers who should ultimately decide on the most appropriate language for describing sensitive topics or identities. As AI becomes more integrated into cataloguing workflows, maintaining a balance between automated processes and human expertise is essential. AI can greatly accelerate the cataloguing of large collections, but the cultural and contextual understanding that cataloguers bring is irreplaceable in guaranteeing inclusivity and ensuring the accuracy and validity of the metadata.

AI also plays a valuable role in supporting inclusive cataloguing by enabling multilingual and multicultural cataloguing processes. With AI models trained on multiple languages, libraries and institutions can catalogue materials from around the world more efficiently and in ways that are both culturally sensitive and linguistically accurate. This capability allows them to better serve diverse, global audiences, ensuring that materials are accessible to people across various language and cultural backgrounds. One powerful example of this is OCR technology, which has advanced significantly in detecting and interpreting scripts beyond the Latin alphabet. In countries like Belgium, where cataloguers primarily work with Latin script, it can be challenging to catalogue materials in languages that use different scripts, such as Arabic, Greek or Chinese. Traditionally, cataloguers might not be trained to read or write in these scripts, making it difficult to accurately record bibliographic details for materials in these languages. However, OCR tools –

such as Microsoft's OCR technology – now recognise a wide range of scripts with ease. This capability makes it significantly easier to create bibliographic records for multilingual materials without requiring specialised language skills. By automating the recognition and transcription of non-Latin scripts, OCR helps bridge language barriers in cataloguing, contributing to a more inclusive and comprehensive library catalogue that reflects the linguistic diversity of a global readership. In this way, AI and OCR technology empower libraries to expand their collections to include a richer variety of languages and cultural perspectives, ultimately fostering a more inclusive and globally representative catalogue.

Traditional cataloguing methods versus modern approaches using AI

Traditional cataloguing

Traditional cataloguing is a highly detailed process in which human cataloguers manually create bibliographic records for each item in a library's collection. The cataloguer physically examines the book or resource, carefully analysing key elements such as the title, author, publication information, subject matter and other relevant details. Using this information, they then apply established cataloguing standards, along with institutional guidelines, to ensure that the record accurately represents the resource. This process requires significant expertise as cataloguers must possess a deep understanding of both the materials they are working with and the cataloguing standards that guide their work. This expertise is essential for maintaining the precision, consistency and accessibility of the library's records.

One of the primary advantages of traditional cataloguing is the invaluable human expertise that shapes each step of the process. Professional cataloguers possess a deep understanding of library science, allowing them to craft detailed, nuanced and highly accurate descriptions of materials. This expertise is especially crucial when cataloguing items that are rare, complex or one-of-a-kind – situations where automated systems often struggle to capture the subtleties or the true significance of a resource. Cataloguers bring a unique ability to recognise subtle distinctions and interpret context, both of which are essential for researchers and scholars who need specific, accurate information. Cataloguers also understand that documents, books and other materials are often the result of creative, artistic or intellectual efforts. Many artists and critical thinkers intentionally challenge societal norms and approach the concept of a book or document in unconventional ways. This diversity of expression can make it challenging to apply rigid rules or formulae to cataloguing. AI systems, while useful in many areas, can't be easily trained to grasp these layers of meaning, symbolism or intention. Human cataloguers, however, can appreciate these nuances, providing richer metadata that reflects the true essence of a work. Through their careful attention to detail, cataloguers ensure that records adhere to the highest standards of accuracy and consistency. This is essential for effective resource discovery and for supporting academic research and maintaining bibliographic control across a library's collection.

One clear and compelling example, drawn from a real-life discussion at KBR, revolves around the seemingly simple question: What are comics? At first glance, the answer might appear straightforward – perhaps something like 'a series of drawings presented in panels, using text balloons to tell a story'. However, defining a comic is far from simple. While there are certain established criteria, the boundaries are often blurred as many creators experiment with form and push the limits of traditional classifications. Consider this: some works feature drawings but omit text balloons entirely, instead relying on visuals alone to convey meaning. Others might incorporate images that resemble fine art or paintings when most comics use line art. Some comic books verge on poetry, focusing on lyrical expression rather than a narrative-driven story. This raises important questions: How do we determine whether a particular work should be classified as a comic book? And further, how do we decide whether it fits within subcategories like US comics, cartoons, graphic novels, fanzines, manga, manhwa or manfra?

The process of classification involves multiple layers of consideration. It is not enough to analyse the visual or structural aspects of the work in isolation. Comics are a specific medium with particular visual and narrative codes and devices but they are also a cultural practice. For example, factors that can determine the classification are: 'Is the publisher known for specialising in comic books?' or 'Is the creator recognised as someone active in the comic industry?' Another factor might be whether the publication is marketed and priced as a comic within its cultural or commercial context. These nuanced questions highlight how classification often extends beyond the content itself, delving into the broader context of production, distribution and intent.

This complexity underscores the need for human expertise. Assigning accurate and meaningful metadata requires careful judgement and a deep understanding of both the medium and its context. While AI can be trained to identify certain patterns or criteria, it struggles with these more subjective, interpretive decisions. For example, distinguishing between a poetic graphic novel and an experimental illustrated text may require insights that only a human can provide – insights shaped by cultural knowledge, historical awareness and the ability to interpret subtle artistic choices. Whether someone is casually exploring a library collection or conducting in-depth academic research, the quality and accuracy of this information directly impact their experience. In an era where the boundaries of creative forms are constantly evolving, maintaining this balance between human judgement and technological support is more important than ever.

On the other hand, traditional cataloguing presents some significant challenges. The process is highly time-consuming and labour-intensive. The meticulous attention to detail, while ensuring accuracy, makes manual cataloguing a slow process. As libraries grow larger and their collections expand, especially in environments like national or university libraries where thousands of new materials are added annually, managing this workload through traditional methods becomes increasingly difficult. Cataloguers can only process a finite number of records each day, which often leads to backlogs and delays in making new resources accessible to users. The sheer volume of materials – ranging from books and manuscripts to digital resources – outpaces the speed at which cataloguers can work. This issue is particularly acute in national and academic libraries, where timely access to new publications is crucial for research and scholarship. As a result, libraries may struggle to maintain up-to-date catalogues, limiting their ability to meet the needs of users who rely on comprehensive and current collections.

The need for skilled professionals who are trained in cataloguing practices adds another layer of complexity. With the declining availability of library and document education programmes, there are fewer opportunities for individuals to gain formal training in these essential areas. This trend means that fewer professionals are entering the field with the specialised knowledge required for roles in library science, document management and information organisation. As these educational programmes become scarcer, the industry faces challenges in ensuring that the next generation of professionals is equipped with the skills needed to maintain high standards in cataloguing, archival work and resource management. This shortage impacts libraries and information centres today and poses long-term implications for preserving and accessing knowledge resources in the future.

Another significant challenge modern libraries face is the reduction in personnel, particularly in cataloguing departments. Many libraries are operating with fewer staff members, including a dwindling number of cataloguers, even as the volume of published materials continues to rise steadily. This shrinking workforce struggles to keep pace with the ever-growing influx of new publications, making it difficult for libraries to manage their collections effectively.

Adding to this complexity is the increasing diversity of materials being published today. Not only are there more books, but they are also being produced in a wider range of languages, scripts and formats than ever before. The growing number of publications in non-Latin alphabets, such as Arabic, Chinese, Cyrillic and others, requires specialised knowledge that many cataloguing departments do not always possess. Handling this linguistic and cultural diversity is a particularly daunting task for national and international libraries, which are often responsible for maintaining comprehensive, inclusive records that reflect the full breadth of global scholarship and literature.

For cataloguers, this means grappling with not just the technical aspects of cataloguing, but also with understanding the context and nuances of materials from different cultures and languages. Ensuring that records are accurate and accessible to a broad audience becomes even more challenging when dealing with multilingual resources. These complexities place additional strain on cataloguing departments, highlighting the need for both specialised skills and sufficient staffing to maintain the high standards that library users expect.

In summary, while traditional cataloguing offers the benefit of human expertise and attention to detail, it is increasingly difficult to scale for large, diverse collections. The demands on cataloguing departments are greater than ever and with fewer resources at their disposal, libraries must explore new solutions to manage their collections more efficiently without compromising the quality of their cataloguing work.

Modern cataloguing using AI

The rise of AI in recent years has marked one of the most transformative technological developments of the 21st century. AI, which encompasses a broad range of technologies enabling machines to perform tasks that typically require human intelligence, has evolved rapidly, driven by advances in computing power, data availability and algorithmic innovation.

The journey of AI began in the mid-20th century with foundational theories and the development of the first AI programs. Early AI research focused on symbolic AI and rule-based systems, where machines followed explicit instructions to perform tasks. However, progress was slow due to limited computational resources and narrow problem domains.

The real turning point in AI's evolution came with the rise of machine learning (ML), a subfield of AI that allows systems to learn from data rather than relying solely on programmed rules. In the 2000s, the advent of large datasets and increased computational power – particularly through graphics processing units (GPUs) – enabled significant breakthroughs. Machine learning techniques, especially deep learning, which uses neural networks with many layers to model complex patterns in data, started showing impressive results. This period saw the development of systems that could recognise speech, identify images and translate languages with unprecedented accuracy.

By the 2010s, AI technologies began to permeate everyday life. Virtual assistants like Siri, Alexa and Google Assistant became commonplace, offering users hands-free control over their devices and services. Recommendation algorithms powered personalised content on platforms such as Netflix and Amazon, while autonomous vehicles, though still in developmental stages, captured the public's imagination with their potential to transform transportation.

The 2020s have witnessed an acceleration in AI capabilities. Large language models (LLMs), such as OpenAI's GPT-3 and its successors, have demonstrated remarkable proficiency in understanding and generating human-like text, enabling applications from chatbots to content creation. These models leverage vast amounts of text data and sophisticated algorithms to perform tasks with a level of coherence and contextual understanding that was previously unattainable. Image creation AI, exemplified by technologies like DALL·E and Midjourney, represents a groundbreaking advancement in the field of artificial intelligence. These systems leverage deep learning models to generate highly detailed and imaginative images based on textual descriptions. For example, DALL-E, also developed by OpenAI, can create visually coherent and contextually relevant images from complex prompts, demonstrating a remarkable ability to combine and synthesise diverse elements into novel compositions. Similarly, Midjourney offers an intuitive platform for users to produce unique, artistic visuals by interpreting and translating text inputs into striking images. These tools expand the possibilities for creative expression and revolutionise industries such as advertising, design and entertainment by enabling rapid, customisable image generation that was once constrained by human limitations.

Looking ahead, the evolution of AI promises even greater advancements. Researchers are exploring new paradigms, such as general AI, which aims to achieve human-like cognitive abilities and quantum computing, which could revolutionise how AI systems process information. The continued development of AI will likely bring about more sophisticated applications and innovations, potentially transforming numerous aspects of life and work.

With this in mind, it is logical that libraries and heritage institutions began exploring how AI could assist in collection management and enhance user experiences. AI technologies offer transformative potential for these institutions by automating routine tasks, improving the organisation and accessibility of vast collections and providing advanced search and recommendation systems. The scalability of AI-driven systems enables the management of increasingly large digital collections, ensuring metadata remains up-to-date (Tait and Pierson, 2022). Semantic enrichment capabilities of AI can enhance user experiences by providing deeper contextual understanding and facilitating the discovery of related resources (Monyela and Tella, 2024). Machine learning algorithms can be used to create personalised recommendations for users based on their interests and previous interactions, making it easier for them to discover relevant materials. By integrating AI into their operations, libraries and heritage institutions can streamline their processes and offer enriched and more engaging experiences for their users.

One of the most impactful contributions of AI in this area is its ability to automate routine cataloguing tasks, such as subject classification, text recognition and, as this book is about, metadata extraction. Traditionally, these tasks required human cataloguers to manually review materials and enter detailed metadata, a time-consuming process with potential variations and occasional inaccuracies over time and across different cataloguers.

One standout tool in the realm of subject indexing is Annif, developed by the National Library of Finland. Annif is an open-source tool that automates the process of indexing subjects using a combination of natural language processing (NLP) and ML technologies like TensorFlow, Omikuji, fastText and Gensim. Its multilingual capability means it supports any subject vocabulary, whether in Simple Knowledge Organization System (SKOS) or tab-separated values (TSV) formats, and it is adaptable to various languages as long as the necessary language tools are available. Annif is versatile, offering a command-line interface, a straightforward web user interface (UI) and a REST API for seamless integration with other systems. Information about Annif and its setup can be found on their GitHub page: https://github.com/NatLibFi/Annif.

Annif is a powerful tool that brings efficiency and innovation to subject indexing, making it a valuable asset for libraries and information centres around the world. A recent article evaluates Annif's application in the Swedish national library for Dewey Decimal Classification (DDC), emphasising the need for semi-automated solutions to improve subject classification in scaling library catalogues and digital collections. The study, using a larger dataset and multiple algorithms (e.g., SVC, fastText, Omikuji), achieved improved accuracy. The article suggests that hierarchical DDC relationships could enhance disambiguation. It calls for further testing, better evaluation standards and performance assessments to determine the value of automated classification in improving document retrieval and discoverability (Golub et al., 2024). The idea of working on a hierarchical level will be discussed later in Chapter 3, where a first model detects a general category, followed by a specific model for more detailed classification.

Optical character recognition (OCR) and handwritten text recognition (HTR) are powerful tools used for text recognition, enabling AI systems to convert scanned images of printed text into machine-readable data. This is particularly useful for unlocking older documents or materials that are not available in digital format. Worth mentioning here is Transkribus (www.transkribus.org). Transkribus enables you to automatically recognise text easily, edit seamlessly, collaborate effortlessly and even train your custom AI for digitising and interpreting historical documents of any form. Transkribus can be used to recognise text from older, handwritten archival or literary documents. You can train custom AI models for text and layout tailored to your specific needs. Additionally, Transkribus enhances your workflow by facilitating metadata enrichment, fostering collaboration and providing powerful full-text search capabilities. Recent research highlights that HTR not only facilitates accurate transcription and dataset cleaning but also enhances access to diverse historical materials, creating a virtuous cycle of dataset production. However, challenges such as reliance on digitisation pipelines, potential archival omissions and entrenched biases persist.

These developments underscore the transformative potential of tools like Transkribus in shaping future information environments and expanding our understanding of the past (Nickels et al., 2024). The integration of tools like Microsoft Power Platform could offer potential solutions to these constraints, providing flexible, low-code frameworks for addressing metadata, collaboration and digitisation processes.

In this book, we will delve into the potential of image-based processing, which goes far beyond the standard capabilities of OCR. While OCR is traditionally used to convert printed text into machine-readable formats, AI-driven image processing takes it a step further by analysing the layout of documents – like a title page – to detect patterns and extract metadata with greater precision. For example, AI can quickly scan elements such as the title, author, publication date and subject matter from a title or copyright page by recognising patterns in the arrangement of text, fonts and design elements.

AI excels at managing large-scale collections with remarkable efficiency, especially those containing materials in a variety of scripts or languages. This capability is particularly advantageous for libraries with diverse collections, such as those that include works in non-Latin scripts. Traditional cataloguing can be a time-consuming and challenging task when it requires human expertise across multiple languages and unfamiliar scripts. AI, however, can be trained to recognise and process these different scripts, ensuring accurate and consistent metadata extraction across a wide range of languages. AI systems recognise these scripts and can apply cataloguing standards uniformly, helping to maintain consistency across multilingual collections. This eliminates many of the hurdles that human cataloguers might face, such as limited language expertise or unfamiliarity with particular writing systems. By handling these complexities with precision, AI makes it easier for libraries to catalogue materials from around the world and provide accurate records for their users, regardless of language.

Integrating AI into the cataloguing process can significantly speed up the initial stages of record creation by automating tasks such as extracting basic metadata, identifying keywords and classifying general topics. However, as noted, generating more complex metadata – like analysing the subtleties of the content or adding precise details about the physical attributes of the book (such as measurements, page count, binding type and other specific characteristics) – remains a task best handled by human professionals. This is because cataloguers bring a level of discernment and appreciation for nuance that AI, at present, can't fully replicate, especially when interpreting intricate or context-rich materials. In a recent article, the authors give an overview of the existing literature and recent trends of AI in libraries (Oyighan et al., 2024). The authors highlight that while AI-driven metadata management offers significant opportunities, it also presents notable challenges. These include maintaining high data quality and consistency, which are critical for ensuring the accuracy of AI-generated metadata. The main challenges are poor metadata quality that can lead to flawed recommendations, ethical and privacy concerns and biases in training datasets (Oyighan et al., 2024, 24–5). While automation can handle a large volume of data, human oversight remains essential in the cataloguing process. Power Apps provides an opportunity to combine AI-driven automation with human input, allowing cataloguers to refine and enhance AI-generated metadata by adding contextual knowledge, correcting errors, and ensuring the accuracy of complex details.

In our retrocataloguing application, we deliberately chose to include a human validation step and this has proven to be a critical part of the process. Incorporating human oversight does not imply that AI-driven metadata extraction is ineffective or that it does not save time. On the contrary, the true value lies in the combination of both – AI for automation, accuracy and efficiency, complemented by human expertise for interpretation and refinement. The most effective approach, therefore, lies in combining the strengths of AI with the irreplaceable expertise of human cataloguers. AI can handle repetitive, time-consuming tasks and swiftly generate initial data, while cataloguers can focus on adding depth and precision to the record. This hybrid method enhances efficiency and ensures that each catalogue entry maintains the quality, accuracy and context necessary to meet the diverse needs of researchers, scholars and casual library users. In this way, the cataloguing process becomes both faster and richer, leveraging AI's capabilities to complement and enhance human insight.

In summary, AI has the potential to revolutionise modern cataloguing by automating routine tasks, enhancing the accuracy and consistency of records and enabling libraries to manage large and diverse collections with greater efficiency. Technologies like OCR, NLP and ML are at the forefront of this transformation, providing libraries with the tools to keep pace with the growing volume and complexity of published materials. AI can scale to accommodate the continuous growth of collections, processing materials quickly and efficiently without compromising accuracy. This is especially important for global institutions, national libraries or research facilities that house vast, multilingual archives. In these environments, AI ensures that diverse collections are catalogued with the same level of thoroughness and standardisation, bridging gaps in language expertise and contributing to a more accessible and well-organised repository of knowledge.

Incorporating AI into cataloguing elevates the quality and reliability of the records, making it an invaluable tool for modern libraries and archives striving to manage and preserve vast amounts of information. As we continue to explore the capabilities of AI, including its potential for image-based processing and pattern recognition, the future of cataloguing looks promising, with AI offering innovative solutions to long-standing challenges.

AI alone is not enough: the importance of automation in library processes

Streamlining cataloguing workflows

Where libraries are managing vast collections and dealing with an influx of newly published materials, streamlining cataloguing workflows has become an essential part of resource management. While AI presents exciting opportunities to automate certain aspects of the cataloguing process, the use of AI and the outcome must be integrated into a larger, structured workflow that encompasses the entire process, from scanning materials to validating the final bibliographic record. AI detection enables automation, which in turn can significantly reduce the manual workload, allowing librarians to focus more on supervisory and strategic tasks. This was also one of the key conclusions highlighted in my presentation at WLIC (Lowagie, 2023a). A holistic approach is key to addressing the growing challenge of handling large collections and a continuous stream of incoming books. AI tools can significantly enhance efficiency, but only when integrated thoughtfully into the workflow. Before going into the details of the solution, this is where Power Platform comes into play, particularly Power Automate. Power Automate plays an important role because it allows you to initiate and automate various steps of the process, ensuring seamless co-ordination between tasks such as metadata extraction, data entry and final validation. By leveraging Power Automate, libraries can automate the entire cataloguing workflow, making it faster and more scalable while still ensuring the quality of bibliographic records.

One of the major benefits of automation in cataloguing workflows is the ability to minimise the amount of manual and repetitive work involved. Tasks like data entry, basic bibliographic description and metadata creation can be handled by AI, freeing up cataloguers to focus on more complex areas that require human judgement, such as subject classification, authority control and entity-cataloguing (adding the levels of work and/or expression). By reducing the burden of routine tasks, AI allows human cataloguers to apply their expertise where it matters most, ensuring the highest quality of cataloguing.

The process of automating cataloguing workflows should be approached incrementally. Automation can begin with basic tasks, such as scanning and metadata extraction, and gradually move toward more complex areas like subject classification and authority control. As each stage is automated, cataloguers and system administrators can assess how effectively AI is performing, making adjustments and improvements as necessary. Each step of automation presents an opportunity for refinement and optimisation.

To successfully implement an efficient automation workflow, it is essential to thoroughly analyse the existing cataloguing workflow in your institution. Each step that a human cataloguer currently performs must be carefully examined to identify opportunities for automation. Start by understanding the initial steps: Where does the book first arrive? How is the arrival registered? Is there an existing system in place for recording arrivals and how can it be streamlined?

Next, consider the process for creating or importing bibliographic records. Is a new record created from scratch or can pre-existing or pre-imported records be utilised? If pre-existing records are available, how are they searched for and retrieved? If pre-existing records are not available, at what point is the bibliographic record generated? This stage-by-stage assessment will highlight where automation can be most effective.

Similarly, analyse the cataloguing process in detail. Ask questions like: Where do cataloguers begin their work? What information do they look up first and where do they find it? By breaking down each action into clear steps, you can methodically evaluate which tasks can be automated and how the overall workflow can be improved.

A step-by-step approach is essential to ensure that every component of the cataloguing process is systematically assessed for potential enhancement. This detailed analysis allows for thoughtful integration of automation, resulting in a more efficient and scalable system without compromising the accuracy and quality of the cataloguing process. We will analyse the different steps and how they are translated into automation in Chapter 4.

Enhancing accuracy and reducing human error

In library cataloguing, maintaining accuracy and minimising human error are essential for ensuring that bibliographic records are reliable and consistent. One of the major advantages of AI-driven cataloguing systems is their ability to minimise human errors that can occur during the metadata entry process.

Automated systems are designed to follow predefined rules and standards without deviation, eliminating common typographical errors and ensuring that metadata is entered correctly. When text recognition and metadata extraction function effectively, AI can quickly generate accurate and standardised metadata, streamlining the cataloguing process and minimising inconsistencies. This increases the overall reliability of the catalogue. Moreover, an automation process can help by automatically verifying information against external databases, cross-referencing details like author names, subject headings or ISBNs, ensuring that the metadata being entered is accurate and up to date. This automated verification process prevents many of the inaccuracies that can occur when cataloguers rely on memory or outdated reference materials.

Consistency is a critical element in cataloguing, particularly in large-scale systems like shared catalogues where multiple institutions contribute to a unified database. In these environments, inconsistent metadata can lead to confusion and hinder users' ability to find resources. Automation flows, whether or not powered by AI, ensure that metadata is applied uniformly across all records by adhering strictly to cataloguing standards and formats.

This is particularly important when cataloguing large volumes of materials, such as books, digital resources or media from different publishers, languages or regions. Automated systems can apply standardised rules across all entries, ensuring that key fields like author names, titles and subject headings are formatted and recorded consistently. In a manual workflow, these fields might vary slightly depending on the individual cataloguer's interpretation. AI ensures a uniform approach, making it easier for users to search and retrieve materials.

To give an example, automation flows can be programmed to follow specific authority control standards, ensuring that every author, subject or publisher is catalogued in exactly the same way across the entire system. This uniformity is vital for maintaining a cohesive catalogue that is easy to navigate, especially in collaborative environments where multiple institutions rely on shared data.

In addition to automating the entry of metadata, components of the automation process can also play a crucial role in validating the data once it has been entered. By incorporating validation steps within the workflow, libraries can ensure that the information being catalogued is accurate, consistent and up to institutional standards.

Incorporating AI into cataloguing workflows offers significant advantages in terms of accuracy and consistency. Automated systems drastically reduce human error, ensure uniformity across large datasets and provide real-time validation of metadata. While AI is not a replacement for human cataloguers, it serves as a powerful tool to enhance their work, allowing them to focus on more complex tasks that require critical thinking and expertise. By leveraging tools like Power Automate, libraries can streamline the entire cataloguing workflow, significantly increasing speed and scalability while maintaining high standards of quality and consistency across bibliographic records. This approach enhances efficiency and safeguards the integrity of the cataloguing process.

The evolving role of the cataloguer

The responsibilities of modern cataloguers are undergoing significant transformation. As AI becomes more integrated into library and information science, cataloguers are now shifting from traditional, manual tasks to a more strategic and supervisory role. Rather than individually handling each book and completing cataloguing tasks item by item, cataloguers are now more focused on managing and enhancing the automated processes that drive cataloguing on a larger scale.

A key aspect of this new role involves working with AI-generated metadata. Cataloguers will have to collaborate with AI systems to enrich, validate and refine the metadata these systems produce. This means that rather than creating metadata from scratch, cataloguers review the output of AI models, assess its quality and make any necessary adjustments to ensure accuracy. Additionally, they play a crucial role in refining the AI models themselves as well as updating and improving the external datasets that these systems rely on for automated searches. In essence, this shift moves cataloguers from a traditional, hands-on role to a higher level position where they are responsible for ensuring the precision and reliability of large-scale automated cataloguing systems.

By overseeing AI-driven processes, cataloguers can now leverage technology to maintain the integrity of information organisation on a broader scale, allowing them to serve the needs of modern libraries and information systems more effectively. As this transition continues, the skills and expertise required of cataloguers will evolve, emphasising digital literacy, data management and AI oversight, alongside traditional knowledge of classification and cataloguing.

Power Platform as a solution

In summary, we are witnessing rapid advancements in AI capabilities, with a wide array of tools and solutions that hold incredible potential. On one hand, we have emerging AI possibilities and, on the other, the need to incorporate them efficiently into cataloguing workflows. For a library manager, data manager or librarian beginning to explore how AI can improve their workflow, the sheer variety of tools, technical skills required and budget considerations can quickly become overwhelming. Even when a suitable AI tool is identified, tested and installed, its effectiveness depends on how well it integrates into the everyday cataloguing processes. Standalone tools, no matter how advanced, will fall short if they are not seamlessly embedded into the workflow. At KBR, we have encountered these same challenges in our own efforts. Each time we tested a promising tool, several questions immediately arose:

- How are we going to use it?
- Who in our institution will maintain that tool?
- Do we need IT support for this?
- Is our IT department willing and able to provide that support?

These concerns arise even before addressing the broader transformation underway in bibliographic standards, such as the transition to Linked Data, moving from MARC to BIBFRAME, implementing RDA cataloguing principles and adding uniform resource identifiers (URIs) where possible. This shift alone is a significant challenge that requires a thoughtful and strategic approach. To address all these needs, we began exploring Microsoft Power Platform as it offered a comprehensive solution to streamline our workflows and integrate a variety of AI capabilities.

Power Platform is not just a single tool; it is a versatile platform that empowers you to design, create and customise tools and workflows tailored specifically to your institution's unique needs. Every organisation – whether a library, archive or heritage institution – has its own set of priorities, operational nuances and specific workflows. A 'one-size-fits-all' tool often fails to meet these varied requirements effectively as it may lack the flexibility to accommodate unique processes or to adapt as needs evolve. This is where the Power Platform's customisable nature offers a significant advantage. Instead of adapting your institution to a rigid, pre-built tool, Power Platform enables you to create a personalised solution that fits seamlessly within your existing operations. With this platform, you are not limited to predefined functionalities. Instead, you have the creative freedom to develop applications, automate tasks and integrate data flows that address your institution's precise goals. This adaptability means that as your organisation grows and its needs change, you can continue to refine and expand the tools you have built on the platform, ensuring they remain relevant and effective. Unlike an out-of-the-box solution that might work for one organisation but fall short for another, Power Platform provides a flexible framework where you can build precisely what you need to address the distinct challenges and demands of your institution.

In the next chapter, we will provide a detailed overview of Power Platform and discuss the specific ways it can enhance cataloguing processes, offering practical insights into its diverse functionalities and benefits.

CHAPTER 2

Getting Started with the Power Platform Ecosystem

Overview of the Power Platform ecosystem

Managing large volumes of data and streamlining workflows has become essential for enterprises, organisations and libraries and heritage institutions. To meet these challenges, the Power Platform ecosystem provides a suite of tools designed to automate processes, facilitate data management and integrate a toolbox of AI models, all without requiring advanced technical expertise. This chapter will introduce you to the Power Platform ecosystem, focusing on how organisations, but especially librarians and archivists, can leverage Microsoft Power Apps, even with limited technical experience, to revolutionise cataloguing workflows. The ecosystem consists of five main components:

1. Power Apps: A cloud-based platform that enables users to build custom applications using a simple, intuitive drag-and-drop interface.
2. Power Automate: Allows users to automate repetitive tasks and workflows, reducing manual effort and freeing up valuable time.
3. Power BI: A powerful business analytics tool that enables users to analyse data, visualise insights and share interactive reports and dashboards with ease.
4. Power Pages: A tool within the Power Platform ecosystem that allows users to create professional, user-friendly websites that can be accessed by individuals outside the organisation.
5. Copilot Studio: An innovative tool that allows users to customise and deploy an AI-assisted chatbot, known as a 'Copilot'.

These tools can all be connected to the following components:

- Dataverse: A scalable, cloud-based data platform that serves as the backbone of the Power Platform ecosystem, allowing users to securely store and manage their data.

- AI Builder or AI Hub: A low-code AI platform that allows users to integrate AI capabilities directly into their apps and workflows within the Power Platform ecosystem.

Power Platform's ease of use makes it an ideal choice for users across various fields who need to develop custom solutions without relying on developers. The tools and components within the Power Platform ecosystem are evolving at a rapid pace. While the information and guidance provided here reflect the current capabilities and interface, it is important to note that Microsoft frequently updates and refines its products. These changes can affect the look, feel or available options within the platform. However, despite these updates, the core concepts and functionality of the Power Platform remain consistent. The key principles of workflow automation, data management and integration will continue to apply, even if specific features or layouts evolve over time. This means that while the tools may change, the fundamental ideas and methods described here will still provide a valuable insight into how to use the platform effectively.

Power Apps

With Power Apps, you can design apps that are specific to your organisation's needs, especially for cataloguing workflows. The platform integrates easily with existing databases and systems, making it highly versatile. Power Apps operates on a low-code/no-code framework, meaning you do not need to be a developer to create functional apps. The platform allows you to choose pre-built templates or start from scratch. You can add predefined end-user modules, data connections and automation features using visual tools, which significantly reduce the complexity of app development. To get started with Power Apps, it is important to become familiar with its interface. When you log into Power Apps, you will be greeted by a dashboard that provides access to all your apps, data connections and environments. When you click on 'New app', you are presented with several options to begin building your application:

- Start with Copilot: This option allows you to describe the type of application you want to build and Copilot, an AI-driven assistant, will generate a proposed application based on your input. This approach is ideal for those who prefer to guide the creation process through natural language as Copilot helps automate the design and functionality, saving time and effort. You can refine the proposal or add specific features as needed.

- Start with data: If you already have a data source, this option lets you begin by connecting your app to that data. You can link the app to existing data from sources like SharePoint lists, Excel spreadsheets, CSV files or even create a new table from scratch. Starting with data is particularly useful when your app's primary purpose is to interact with, display or modify existing datasets.
- Start with a page design: This option provides you with a range of pre-designed page templates to choose from. You can select layouts for different types of screens, such as forms, dashboards or galleries and then customise them to suit your specific needs. It is a quick way to start building visually appealing pages without having to design everything from the ground up.
- Start with an app template: Here, you can choose from a variety of pre-made applications designed for specific use cases, such as SAP Procurement, Employee Kudos, Awards and Recognitions, Hardware Request and Management or Onboarding Buddy. These templates offer a ready-made structure that you can modify to match your organisation's needs, providing a fast-track solution for common business processes.

Once you start with a blank Power App, you are ready to begin creating your own custom application. Power Apps provides an intuitive platform where you can easily add various elements to bring your app to life. For example, you can insert buttons for navigation, icons for visual appeal, galleries to display data or even media files, such as images and videos, to enhance the user experience. Each of these components can be customised based on the functionality you want to provide. You can define what each button does, whether it is submitting a form, navigating to another screen or triggering a specific action within the app. This is done through a simple, user-friendly interface that allows you to insert actions, commands and logic behind every element with minimal effort. For example, by selecting a button, you can configure it to save data, filter a gallery or perform other complex operations based on user input. This drag-and-drop approach to app development makes it incredibly easy to build powerful applications without needing extensive coding knowledge. As you continue to add elements, you will start to see your app taking shape.

One of the key strengths of Power Apps is its ability to connect to a variety of data sources:

- SharePoint Lists: SharePoint Lists are essentially collections of information that can be shared and collaborated on within a SharePoint site. SharePoint Lists are similar to databases but are designed to integrate with other Microsoft 365 tools. A SharePoint List consists of columns (which define the types of data stored, such as text, numbers, dates or choices) and rows (which are individual records or entries within the list).

- SharePoint Document Library: Power Apps can pull in data or images from SharePoint to use in the application.
- Dataverse: For more robust and scalable data management, Dataverse provides a secure and centralised database platform (see below for more information).
- Excel: You can connect directly with an Excel file on your SharePoint or OneDrive, allowing the app to read, update and interact with the data. This is ideal for smaller libraries or departments that use Excel for simple cataloguing tasks.

Once you are satisfied with the design and functionality of your app, you can save it. Saving the app is just the first step. To make it accessible to others, you need to publish it. This allows you to share the app with your team or organisation, ensuring that everyone can use it seamlessly. Once published, the app becomes live and can be used by others on any device, whether it is a mobile phone, tablet or desktop. Power Apps enables you to quickly turn ideas into functional tools that boost productivity and streamline internal processes. Its flexibility, scalability and integration with various data sources and the Microsoft ecosystem make it a powerful solution for improving workflow efficiency.

Power Automate

Power Automate allows users to automate repetitive tasks and streamline workflows across various applications and services. It is designed to make the automation of processes accessible to people with or without technical backgrounds. Power Automate can handle everything from simple automation tasks, such as sending notifications and e-mails, updating records or generating reports, which would otherwise require significant manual intervention, to more complex workflows that integrate with external systems, databases or even AI components.

Every automated workflow or 'flow', within Power Automate requires a trigger to start the process. This trigger could be something simple like clicking a button in Power Apps or more complex, such as the creation of a new file in OneDrive or SharePoint. This offers significant opportunities for automation in various scenarios. For example, when a new scan is created, it can trigger the flow and start the document processing or the cataloguing process.

One of Power Automate's greatest strengths is its ability to connect and integrate with numerous platforms and applications. The possibilities are extensive and cover many routine tasks, such as sending data or images directly to an e-mail via Outlook, adding information to an Excel spreadsheet, creating files in OneDrive or SharePoint or sharing information across teams, all automatically triggered and executed. Power Automate also enables advanced users to perform HTTP requests – allowing actions like POST, GET, PUT and DELETE through API calls. This feature is particularly useful for interacting with external data sources or updating records in systems that Power Automate might not natively support. By integrating with external APIs, users can push data to other systems, fetch information and even synchronise databases, extending the functionality of automated workflows beyond the immediate Microsoft ecosystem.

Another component of Power Automate that will be useful for cataloguing tasks is its ability to interact with file transfer protocol (FTP) and SFTP servers. The SFTP/FTP component allows users to create files on external servers. This can be useful, for example, for sending the bibliographic records to the servers of a library management system (LMS), which then processes the uploaded file and creates a bibliographic record using the LMS's import function. This is a highly effective way to streamline workflows in situations where manual file uploads are time-consuming.

Finally, Power Automate provides seamless integration with AI models, allowing users to deploy custom AI models to process data or images within their workflows. You can trigger an AI model directly within a flow to analyse documents, classify images or extract information. This feature will be explored in detail in Chapter 3, where we discuss how to build and implement AI components into Power Automate flows to enhance automation capabilities.

Power Automate offers basic and premium components. Standard features are included as part of the Microsoft 365 license, providing users with essential tools and functionalities for everyday tasks. However, certain advanced features and capabilities require a premium license. For example, if you need to perform HTTP requests or integrate AI components, a premium account is required. These premium features offer enhanced functionality, such as more advanced automation, customisations and integrations. Details about these premium features, along with the specific licensing requirements, are covered in the next part. Once you have premium access, the range of features expands significantly, including the ability to connect with premium partners. These external services, integrated directly into Power Automate, offer even more robust functionality, however they typically require an API key or authentication from the external platform.

Power BI

Power BI is a powerful business analytics tool that enables users to analyse data, visualise insights and easily share interactive reports and dashboards. Designed to integrate seamlessly with the Microsoft ecosystem, Power BI allows users to pull data from a wide range of sources, such as Dataverse, Excel and SQL databases. This flexibility makes it an invaluable tool for creating dynamic reports that provide real-time insights into organisational performance.

With its intuitive interface and robust analytical capabilities, Power BI empowers organisations to make informed, data-driven decisions. Users can identify trends, monitor key performance indicators and explore their data in new ways to uncover valuable insights. The tool supports continuous improvement by offering a clear and customisable view of operational data, helping teams to quickly identify areas that need attention and track progress over time. Additionally, Power BI's sharing capabilities make it easy to collaborate across departments, ensuring that critical insights reach the right people at the right time. By enabling users to transform raw data into actionable insights, Power BI helps organisations optimise their operations and stay competitive in a data-driven world. For example, Power BI can be used to analyse the output of AI models.

Power Pages

Power Pages enables users to create professional, user-friendly websites designed for external audiences. It provides a simple yet flexible solution for organisations looking to share data with individuals outside their internal systems. With Power Pages, users can design custom web interfaces that allow external users to view, search and interact with data stored in Dataverse, SharePoint, Microsoft Dynamics 365 (Virtual Tables) or Microsoft Power BI. Power Pages simplifies the process of sharing data securely with external audiences.

This tool is particularly valuable for organisations needing to share information securely while maintaining a polished and accessible web presence. For example, libraries that lack an OPAC can use Power Pages to provide public access to their catalogue, offering a user-friendly platform for browsing and searching library resources. The process of setting up these web interfaces is streamlined, ensuring that even users without extensive technical expertise can create secure, professional-looking websites.

By simplifying the way organisations share data with external audiences, Power Pages allows users to focus on improving user experience and expanding access to important information, all while maintaining control over the security and integrity of their data.

Copilot Studio

Copilot is a chatbot that can be integrated into apps or websites to assist users by answering questions, providing recommendations or guiding them through various processes. By using AI to power these interactions, Copilot can provide real-time assistance based on user inputs and data stored in connected systems like Dataverse. For libraries, Copilot could serve as a virtual assistant on their website, helping users search for materials, find information about services or troubleshoot common issues. With the ability to be customised for specific tasks, Copilot enhances user experience by providing immediate, intelligent support, reducing the burden on staff while ensuring that users have access to the information they need when they need it.

Dataverse

Dataverse is a scalable, cloud-based data platform that forms the foundation of the Microsoft Power Platform ecosystem. It enables organisations to securely store, manage and structure their data in a unified manner, making it easier to connect and share information across various applications and workflows. By creating a centralised data environment, Dataverse simplifies data management and ensures that different tools within the Power Platform can seamlessly interact with one another. One of the key strengths of Dataverse is its ability to integrate with a wide range of services and data sources, including Excel, SharePoint and third-party platforms, providing flexibility to adapt to the specific needs of any organisation. Whether it is customer data, operational metrics or external inputs, Dataverse allows businesses to bring diverse datasets together under a single umbrella, eliminating silos.

Security is a top priority in Dataverse, which offers robust protection mechanisms to safeguard sensitive information. Organisations can set detailed permissions, control access levels and ensure that data is only accessible to authorised users ('security roles'). This ensures that while data is easily shared across applications and workflows, it remains protected from unauthorised access or breaches. Built-in data governance features also help maintain data quality and compliance with regulatory requirements, making Dataverse a reliable choice for organisations in industries where security and privacy are paramount.

Dataverse's flexibility also extends to its ability to scale as an organisation grows. As data needs evolve, the platform can handle increased volumes and more complex data structures, ensuring it remains a valuable asset regardless of the size or complexity of the business. This adaptability makes Dataverse a long-term solution that grows alongside an organisation, offering the reliability and agility needed in today's fast-paced, data-driven world. In essence, Dataverse serves as the backbone of a connected, integrated data environment, allowing businesses to maximise the value of their data while maintaining the highest levels of security, flexibility and scalability.

As KBR will be using Dataverse more extensively for our cataloguing application, it is possible to provide some additional details. When creating a table in Dataverse, you will need to define the specific fields for each table, adapting them to the type of data you want to store. Dataverse offers various field types to ensure your data is captured accurately and efficiently. An overview can be found here: https://learn.microsoft.com/en-us/power-apps/maker/data-platform/types-of-fields. The different Data Types are:

- Text: Single line of text: With possible formats: Plain text, Text area, Phone number, E-mail, Ticker symbol, URL. Ideal for brief entries such as titles, author names or other concise information.
- Text: Multiple lines of text: Used for longer descriptions or notes, such as detailed summaries or extended metadata.
- Number: With possible formats: Whole number, Decimal, Float, Language code, Duration, Time Zone.
- Date and time: With possible formats: Date and time or Date only.
- Choice: Yes/No: A simple binary choice, useful for fields requiring a straightforward 'yes' or 'no' answer.
- Choice: Choice: Linked to predefined options: This field allows you to create a list of predefined options for users to select from, which is particularly helpful for fields like genres, languages or formats.
- Currency: Currency columns in Dataverse allow organisations to work with multiple currencies and perform calculations using a base currency.
- File: File: The File column in Dataverse is designed to store binary data. It enhances performance by not saving this data in the relational data store, which also reduces storage capacity usage. The default maximum file size is 32 MB, but it can be increased to 131 MB per column as needed.
- File: Image: Gives the user the possibility to store and display images. Images must be less than 30 MB. Formats allowed are jpg, jpeg, gif, bmp and png. This can be used to save book covers and the scans of the title or copyright page or back cover. By defining these fields thoughtfully, you can ensure that your Dataverse tables capture all necessary

information in a structured and organised manner, which in turn supports efficient cataloguing and retrieval processes.

When setting up tables for organising library data, it is important to carefully consider the structure and relationships within your dataset. You have the option to arrange your data across multiple tables, each with well-defined relationships that connect specific fields. Like any other database, you can relate entities one-to-one, one-to-many or many-to-many. This approach can be especially effective in capturing and organising a wide range of details across different categories. For example, a 'Book' table could include fields for essential metadata like title, ISBN, publication date, author and publisher. Meanwhile, an 'Author' table might store details such as name, birth date, nationality and a list of associated works. In platforms like Dataverse, you can create links between these tables, making sure that all related information is interconnected and easy to navigate. This relational structure enhances data accessibility and provides a comprehensive view of each catalogue record. For example, by establishing a relationship between the 'Author' column in the 'Books' table with a related record in the 'Authors' table, you can associate each author with their works, reflecting real-world connections and creating a seamless user experience for anyone browsing the catalogue. For KBR's specific retrocataloguing project, we chose a simpler approach: a single table containing all the data, with no related tables. This decision was influenced by the type of materials we were working with – primarily books by various authors – where separating authors into a different table wouldn't add significant value. Additionally, since our objective was to produce a CSV file, introducing more complexity with multiple tables was unnecessary. In light of these considerations, it is worth trying this approach for projects with similar goals, especially when simplicity and efficiency are top priorities. By focusing on a straightforward data structure, you can achieve a clean, functional setup that meets project needs without the overhead of a more intricate database design.

Once your Dataverse tables and data models are in place, the next step is to connect Dataverse to Power Apps. Through Power Apps, you can design interfaces that allow users to easily search, input and validate catalogue records in Dataverse. Connecting Power Apps to Dataverse allows for dynamic, real-time interactions with your data. This integration ensures that all changes made in Power Apps are immediately reflected in Dataverse, maintaining a unified system that is always up to date.

AI Builder

AI Builder, also known as AI Hub, is a powerful service that allows organisations to seamlessly integrate AI capabilities into their apps and workflows. This tool empowers organisations to enhance their automation processes by adding intelligent features, such as natural language processing, image recognition and predictive analytics, making day-to-day operations smarter and more efficient. With AI Builder, organisations can easily incorporate AI-driven functionalities to streamline complex tasks. For example, libraries can leverage AI Builder to automate metadata extraction from documents, classify materials or even predict user borrowing patterns. This makes cataloguing faster and more accurate, while also improving user interactions by anticipating user needs. The AI-powered automation reduces the manual workload, allowing staff to focus on higher value tasks and delivering an enhanced experience for users.

One of the key strengths of AI Builder is its flexibility. It offers a variety of pre-built AI models that can be quickly deployed for common tasks, such as form processing or object detection. These models can also be customised to fit the specific requirements of an organisation. In cases where the pre-built models do not fully address a unique challenge, users have the option to create their own AI models from scratch ('custom models'). This ensures that AI Builder can adapt to a wide range of industries and use cases, providing tailored solutions to meet each organisation's distinct needs. By integrating AI capabilities into workflows, AI Builder helps organisations work smarter and more efficiently, improving overall productivity and user experience. The capabilities of AI Builder are sufficient for basic AI functions, but more advanced AI solutions can be developed on the Azure AI platform.

In the next chapter, we will explore the AI possibilities within the Microsoft Power Platform in greater detail, shedding light on how AI tools can transform business operations.

Power Platform licensing

Microsoft Power Platform's licensing model is designed with flexibility in mind, offering several plans to cater for diverse organisational needs and usage patterns. Any user or device that interacts with Power Apps, Power Automate, Copilot Studio or Power Pages must have the appropriate license. This ensures that every interaction with the platform, regardless of the method or level of access, complies with licensing requirements. Licenses for using Power Apps, Power Automate, Copilot Studio and Power Pages can be acquired in several ways, depending on the needs of the organisation or individual users. These use rights are available through the Power Platform subscription licenses, which provide full access to the platform's capabilities. Additionally, there are Power Platform subscription add-on licenses that allow users to extend or enhance their existing licenses, as well as pay-as-you-go options for organisations looking for more flexible, usage-based billing models. This provides a range of licensing solutions to suit different usage patterns and business needs.

In Table 2.1 below, the various licensing options are listed to help you choose the most appropriate plan. As of the end of 2024, this is the current situation, but it is important to note that licensing details may evolve over time and changes could occur in the coming years. This part is based on the Microsoft Power Platform Licensing Guide from December 2024. Keeping track of any updates or adjustments to the licensing model is essential to ensure continued alignment with your organisation's needs. The latest information can be found at https://learn.microsoft.com/en-us/power-platform/admin/pricing-billing-skus.

Table 2.1 *Power Platform licensing options*

Power Platform subscription licenses	Power Apps	Power Apps Premium
		Power Apps per app
	Power Automate	Power Automate Premium
		Power Automate per user
		Power Automate Process
		Power Automate per flow
	Copilot Studio	Copilot Studio
	Power Pages	Power Pages Authenticated users
		Power Pages Anonymous users
Power Platform subscription add-on licenses	Power Automate Process Mining add-on	
	Power Automate Hosted RPA add-on	
	Power Automate unattended RPA add-on	
	AI Builder capacity add-on	
	Dataverse Database capacity add-on	
	Dataverse File capacity add-on	
	Dataverse Log capacity add-on	
	Power Platform Requests add-on	
Power Platform pay-as-you-go meters	Power Apps per app meter	
	Power Pages Authenticated users meter	
	Power Pages Anonymous users meter	
	Dataverse Database capacity meter	
	Dataverse File capacity meter	
	Dataverse Log capacity meter	

Rather than go into detail about each of the available licensing options, we will focus specifically on the licenses that are most relevant and useful for the cataloguing application. By narrowing the discussion to the licenses that directly impact this particular use case, we can better understand which options will provide the necessary features and functionality without being overwhelmed by less relevant choices. This will help ensure we select the most suitable licensing model for a cataloguing application's requirements.

Power Apps Premium license

This license is calculated per user per month and users have the ability to run an unlimited number of apps. Additionally, this license allows you to execute all Power Automate flows that are triggered within the app's context. This means you can run flows directly from the app, whether it is initiated by pressing a button or by setting up an automated timer that triggers the flow at regular intervals (for example, every few seconds).

The Power Apps Premium license also includes 500 AI credits, which can be used for using the AI models from AI Builder, which do not need a large amount of AI processing power. (If you need more AI power, you can take a look at the 'AI Builder capacity add-on' (see below).) For smaller organisations with minimal AI needs, a single Power Apps Premium license might be sufficient. For example, in a small library, one Power Apps Premium account used by the librarian could be enough to cover all operational requirements, including app management and automation. Note, though, that the AI Builder credits must be assigned to an environment in order to enable the AI Builder features. Without assigning these credits, you will not be able to access or use the AI Builder tools within that environment.

Power Apps per app license

This license is calculated per user/app/month. It allows individual users to run one custom application or access one Power Pages website, using the full capabilities of Power Apps. This licensing option is particularly appealing for organisations or users who only need to run one or a limited number of apps or websites, but used by multiple persons.

Power Apps per app meter license (pay-as-you-go)

This license is calculated per active user/app/month. It allows individual users to run a single custom application, offering a flexible and cost-efficient licensing model. With this plan, businesses pay for a full month of access, allowing the user to log in and use the app as many times as they want during that period. However, in months when the user does not log in, no charges are incurred. This is especially useful for applications that are not in constant use but may be needed only a few times a year. This usage-based billing ensures that organisations pay solely for active users, rather than committing to a flat rate for all potential users regardless of their actual engagement. It is an ideal solution for organisations looking to control costs while still maintaining the flexibility to provide full access to Power Apps for the necessary users whenever they need it.

Power Automate Premium license

This license is calculated per user/month. Power Automate Premium for individual users provides licensed access to advanced automation capabilities. It enables users to automate workflows in both modern and legacy applications. For modern applications, automation is achieved through API-based digital process automation (cloud flows), allowing seamless interaction with cloud services. For legacy systems, users can implement UI-based robotic process automation (desktop flows) in attended mode, enabling automation of manual, repetitive tasks directly on the desktop. This combination of cloud and desktop automation ensures a versatile, powerful solution for streamlining processes across a variety of platforms and applications. Included in this license are an unlimited number of cloud flows and one bot Desktop flow.

Power Automate Premium offers additional features, including access to AI Builder for advanced scenarios, such as forms processing, object detection, predictions, text classification and text recognition (5,000 credits per month are included). It also allows users to run an attended Robotic Process Automation (RPA) bot on a workstation, streamlining workflows that require human interaction.

If your flow is linked to a canvas or model-driven app in Power Apps, you typically do not need a separate Power Automate license. The licensing requirements depend on the type of Power Apps license you hold:

- Power Apps per app license: This license provides access to a limited set of Power Automate capabilities. Users with this license can use the flow once it is associated with the app.
- Power Apps per user license: This license grants access to flows triggered by a Power Apps action.

- Dynamics 365 license: When the flow is part of a Dynamics 365 app, it must be associated with the app. The owner requires either a Power Apps Premium license or a Dynamics 365 license.

In short, as long as the flow is associated with the app and you have the appropriate Power Apps or Dynamics 365 license, no additional standalone Power Automate license is needed. However, it is also possible to opt for a solution without Power Apps, where automation processes, such as scanning documents, generating files or adding rows to an Excel spreadsheet, are handled solely by Power Automate. Choosing between Power Apps and Power Automate depends on several factors, such as the specific workflow your organisation needs, the available budget and the number of staff involved in the process. Each option has its own benefits and the right decision will vary based on the desired functionality and resources.

Power Automate per user license

This license is calculated per user/month. It enables individual users to create and run unlimited workflows and business processes tailored to their specific needs. This license is designed to encourage widespread adoption of automation within an organisation. When an organisation adopts the per user license across all users, it minimises administrative overheads by eliminating the need to track the number of flows being activated and used. There are no AI credits included in this license.

Power Automate Process license

This license is calculated per bot/month. Power Automate Process licenses a single 'automation' bot or critical business process that can be used to automate a process via robotic process automation in unattended fashion or UI-based digital process automation. Unlike the per user license, the Power Automate Process license can be used by all users within the organisation, providing a solution that supports shared automation across teams without needing individual licenses for each user. It includes 5,000 AI Builder credits.

AI Builder capacity add-on

AI Builder operates on a capacity-based licensing model, where capacity is represented as 'service credits'. These credits act as a universal currency for all AI Builder functionalities. Prerequisites for AI Builder usage include licenses like Power Apps Premium, Power Apps per app, Power Automate

Premium, Power Automate Hosted RPA add-ons and Dynamics 365 Finance subscriptions. If the AI credits included in these licenses are insufficient – such as when you need to process a larger volume of documents – additional AI Builder capacity can be purchased through add-ons, available in capacity packs. Each pack provides one million service credits per month. These credits are pooled across your organisation and usage of AI Builder services draws from the available pool. For example, if your estimated monthly usage is 4.7 million service credits, you would need to purchase five capacity packs to meet that demand.

Different AI Builder functions consume service credits at varying rates, such as forms processing or prediction models. You can consult the AI Builder rate card to better understand how credits are used and to determine the appropriate number of capacity packs for your specific needs. The key rates for AI Builder usage are as follows: Document processing prediction, needed for analysing the content of a title or copyright page, costs 100 credits per document. Text recognition costs 3 credits per image. For a single book, where you scan both the title and copyright pages, along with text recognition from the back cover, the total cost amounts to 203 credits (100+100+3). If you purchase an AI Builder capacity add-on of one million credits, you can calculate the price per credit and thus the price for processing a book. With one million credits, you could process up to 4,926 books per month.

Power Apps Developer Plan

In addition to the trial plans, there's also a free Power Apps Developer Plan. This is a special plan that allows individual self-service sign up and provides an individual environment that the user can use to build apps and flows. These environments show up on the administrator's list of environments with the environment type listed as 'Developer'. The environments are for individual use, so there's no ability to share with other users. Users in your organisation can self-service sign up for this plan even if they have Power Apps and Power Automate license entitlements via another licensing plan. Apps or flows created in a Power Apps Developer environment can't be used by other people in your organisation.

CHAPTER 3

Integrating Artificial Intelligence

Introduction to Microsoft AI Builder

AI Builder is a powerful tool within the Power Platform that allows organisations to integrate AI into their apps and workflows with ease. Designed to be user-friendly, it enables users to add AI capabilities without needing deep technical or coding knowledge and it can assist in a variety of tasks. It offers both prebuilt models, which are ready to use out-of-the-box, and custom models that can be tailored to your specific needs. Below is an overview of the various model categories available in AI Builder.

Documents

Documents are a key source of structured and unstructured data and AI Builder offers several models to extract valuable information from them.

Document processing (custom model)

This custom model enables you to extract specific information from various types of documents, whether they are structured or unstructured. It offers a high degree of flexibility, allowing you to define the exact data you want to retrieve based on your specific needs. Given its adaptability, this is the model KBR uses for extracting data from title and copyright pages. For a more detailed explanation on how to train and use this model effectively, please refer to the next section of this book, where we will explore its functionality in depth.

Invoice processing (prebuilt)

This is a prebuilt document processing model to extract essential data from invoices, such as the invoice ID, customer details, vendor details, ship to address, bill to address, total, tax, subtotal and line items. This type of invoice management is widely used in business settings. Many other tools on the market provide similar data extraction services specifically designed for invoices. These services are popular because they streamline financial processes.

Text recognition (OCR) (prebuilt)

This model uses OCR to extract all the text from photos and PDF documents. It is particularly useful for digitising printed documents.

Receipt processing (prebuilt)

Specifically designed to extract details from receipts, this prebuilt model pulls out information such as the merchant name, address, phone number and the list of purchased items, making it easier to automate expense tracking.

Identity document reader (prebuilt)

This model extracts important data from identity documents such as passports or driving licenses. It can automate the onboarding process by reading personal information from scanned identity documents.

Business card reader (prebuilt)

Ideal for professionals managing large numbers of contacts, this model extracts contact details from business cards and stores them in a structured format, such as a contact management app.

Text

Text data is another crucial resource in many workflows and AI Builder offers several tools to analyse and extract valuable insights from text. Output is always in structured machine-readable data (JSON, Array). Some models may not be supported in every language, therefore it's important to stay up to date with the latest information regarding language support. Microsoft frequently updates and enhances its language offerings, so check online for the most current details. You can find the latest information on supported languages and models on the official Microsoft website, particularly on the Microsoft Learn platform at https://learn.microsoft.com.

Sentiment analysis (prebuilt)

The prebuilt sentiment analysis model is designed to identify whether text data conveys a positive, negative or a 'mixed' sentiment. This tool can be applied to various types of content, including social media posts, customer reviews and any other text-based data you wish to analyse. The sentiment for the entire document is determined by aggregating the scores of individual sentences, allowing for a nuanced understanding of the overall tone. This means that even if some sentences express positivity and others negativity, the model can accurately reflect this complexity in its assessment, making it a valuable resource for businesses and researchers seeking deeper insights into customer feedback and public opinion.

Category classification (prebuilt)

This model classifies customer feedback or other text data into predefined categories, helping businesses quickly organise and respond to input. It is trained for customer feedback so the predefined categories are limited to 'Issues', 'Compliment', 'Customer Service', 'Documentation', 'Price & Billing' and 'Staff'.

Category classification (custom model)

If the prebuilt category classification does not suit your needs, the custom model allows you to define and classify text data into categories tailored to your specific requirements. As it is a custom model, you will need to provide your own training data. For this model, training typically involves a dataset with two columns: Column A contains the categories you want to assign and Column B contains the corresponding text related to each category. This model is particularly useful for automating tasks like subject indexing, which we will explore in more detail later in the book. Combined with the sentiment analysis model, hotel reviews, for example, can be analysed and classified, such as identifying a 'positive' (sentiment analysis) review about 'breakfast' (category classification).

Entity extraction (prebuilt)

This model extracts key elements from text, such as names, dates and locations, and classifies them into predefined categories, simplifying data analysis. Supported entity types are Age, Boolean, City, Colour, Continent, Country or region, Date and time, Duration, E-mail, Event, Language, Money, Number, Ordinal, Organisation, Percentage, Person name, Phone number, Speed, State Street address, Temperature, URL, Weight, Zip code (US format).

Entity extraction (custom model)

AI Builder entity extraction models are designed to identify specific pieces of data within text based on your unique requirements. By recognising key elements, these models classify the extracted information into predefined categories, which can significantly streamline data management processes. This capability is particularly valuable because it allows you to transform unstructured data, such as free-text documents, e-mails or reports, into structured data that is machine-readable and easier to analyse. Once the data is structured, you can apply various processing techniques to retrieve essential information.

Key phrase extraction (prebuilt)

By extracting the most relevant words and phrases from a body of text, this model helps to summarise large documents and identify key themes. It does not attribute a general classification, it only extracts words and phrases and sends them back as machine-readable data. For this reason, it can't assist with subject indexing as it may not always capture the finer details or meaning that subject indexing requires. Let's look at an example based on this passage from Wikipedia about *Harry Potter and the Philosopher's Stone*:

> Harry Potter and the Philosopher's Stone is a fantasy novel written by the British author J. K. Rowling. It is the first novel in the Harry Potter series and was Rowling's debut novel. It follows Harry Potter, a young wizard who discovers his magical heritage on his eleventh birthday when he receives a letter of acceptance to Hogwarts School of Witchcraft and Wizardry. Harry makes close friends and a few enemies during his first year at the school. With the help of his friends, Ron Weasley and Hermione Granger, he faces an attempted comeback by the dark wizard Lord Voldemort, who killed Harry's parents but failed to kill Harry when he was just 15 months old.
>
> (https://en.wikipedia.org/wiki/Harry_Potter_and_the_Philosopher%27s_Stone)

The extracted texts for this sample are (separated by commas): J. K. Rowling, Harry Potter series, fantasy novel, British author, first novel, debut novel, young wizard, magical heritage, eleventh birthday, first year, Ron Weasley, Hermione Granger, dark wizard, Lord Voldemort, Hogwarts School, close friends, Philosopher, Stone, letter, acceptance, Witchcraft, Wizardry, enemies, help, comeback, parents. These results can help in understanding the text's content but are too extensive to be used in a cataloguing context.

Language detection (prebuilt)

This prebuilt model detects the predominant language of a text document. It is especially useful for businesses operating in multilingual environments.

Text translation (prebuilt)

AI Builder supports the translation of text into over 90 languages (mostly the same as the tool mentioned above). This feature allows organisations to seamlessly interact with international clients or documents in different languages.

Structured data

AI Builder also supports structured data, helping users make sense of historical data and forecast future outcomes.

Prediction (custom model)

AI Builder prediction models analyse patterns in historical data and use those patterns to predict future outcomes. By training the model to recognise these patterns, AI Builder can then apply that knowledge to new data, helping you forecast results and make informed decisions. The prediction model can answer business questions in three ways:

1. Binary Predictions: This type of prediction is used when a question has only two possible outcomes, such as yes/no, true/false or pass/fail. Some examples of binary prediction use cases include: Is an applicant eligible for membership? Is this transaction likely to be fraudulent? Is a customer a good candidate for a marketing campaign? Will an account pay their invoices on time?
2. Multiple Outcome Predictions: This type of prediction applies when the question can have more than two possible outcomes. For example: Will a shipment arrive early, on time, late or very late? Which product would a customer be most interested in?
3. Numerical Predictions: This type of prediction answers questions that require a numerical value. Examples include: How many days will it take for a shipment to arrive? How many items should we keep in stock? How many leads should a sales team convert in a month?

By leveraging AI Builder's predictive capabilities, businesses can gain insights that help them prepare for various scenarios and make data-driven decisions.

Images

Images often contain valuable information and AI Builder provides a range of tools to help extract and analyse this data.

Text recognition (OCR) (prebuilt)

This model can extract all text from images and PDF documents. It is perfect for converting printed materials into editable and searchable formats. At KBR, we use this model to extract text from the back cover of a book. The back cover often provides valuable information about the book's content, such as a summary, themes or details about the author. This information can be incredibly useful in helping to better understand and interpret a book, offering insights that may not be immediately apparent from the title or other sources. By analysing this text, we can gain a deeper perspective on the book's relevance, audience and key messages.

Object detection (custom model)

This custom model allows you to train AI to recognise specific objects in images. For example, it can identify inventory items, logos or machinery parts, streamlining tasks like inventory management or visual inspections.

Image description (prebuilt)

This model generates a description of an image, making it easier to catalogue or tag photos with relevant information.

Setting up the document processing model

Document processing is a key AI capability designed to streamline and automate the extraction of structured data from unstructured documents. For the KBR project, where we aim to extract information from images – such as scans of books or the copyright page – the Document Processing model is the model to use. Therefore, it is essential to understand how to create an effective document processing model.

The process of creating and training the model involves several key steps and each step can significantly impact the overall quality of the final model. It is crucial to break down these steps in detail and follow a clear, structured procedure to ensure the best possible outcome. Creating a document processing model is a dynamic and ongoing process that requires attention to detail, careful planning and constant evaluation. By following a systematic procedure and being prepared to make adjustments as needed, you can develop a model that effectively extracts the information from scanned images. This section will guide you through the setup process, from configuring the model to training it for optimal accuracy.

Choose the type of documents

First, it is important to determine whether the documents you are working with are *fixed template documents* (such as forms, invoices or standardised reports), *general documents* (without a fixed structure) or *invoices*. Fixed template documents typically have a consistent layout and structure, with predictable fields for information, such as dates, names and amounts. These documents follow a well-defined layout pattern, making them easier for a model to process because the model can rely on the consistent placement of elements. In contrast, general documents tend to have more variability in their structure and do not follow a rigid format. This variability requires the model to be more flexible and capable of recognising different content structures across different documents. Understanding the type of document you are working with is crucial because it will influence the design and training of the document processing model. Each type presents its own challenges and opportunities for automation.

If you are working with documents that have a consistent title page layout, such as theses from the same university, you can categorise them as 'Fixed template documents'. In many cases, universities require students to follow a specific template or structure for their thesis, meaning the title page will look the same across all submissions. The same applies to books published in a series, where the title page and overall structure may follow a consistent format. However, most projects will involve more variable documents, such as a collection of books that are randomly selected or not published within a series. In these cases, the title pages may differ in design, layout and content, making it harder to rely on a fixed template approach. Since title pages can have various structures and formatting styles, it would be more appropriate to select the 'General documents' option for processing. This option accommodates different layouts and designs, making it suitable for a broader range of documents that do not follow a single, consistent template.

Select the information to extract

Once you've chosen the document type, decide which fields you want to extract. These can include:

- Text fields: For capturing general text such as title, subtitle, place, author names, edition statement and so on.
- Number fields: For extracting numerical data.
- Date fields: For identifying dates.
- Checkboxes: For detecting binary choices, such as yes/no fields.
- Tables: For extracting structured data, such as tables of contents or lists.

Choosing the correct field type is a crucial step in setting up your model effectively. For example, when extracting a publication date, it might seem logical to use a number field since most publication years are simply four-digit numbers or a date field. However, this is not always the case. Sometimes, the publication date may include more than just a year; it could also contain a month or a season, such as 'Spring 2024'. In such cases, opting for a text field instead of a number or date field is a more flexible solution. This allows the model to capture not only the year but also any additional information. By carefully selecting the appropriate field type, you can ensure that your model handles variations in document formats with precision. Opting for a number field or a date field, however, offers valuable advantages when it comes to data searching. For example, using these fields would enable more advanced search capabilities, such as 'show all books published after the year 2000'. Such searches are not feasible with a text field, which limits the ability to perform numerical or date-based queries. Therefore, the choice between a text field and a number or date field should balance flexibility with the specific search and data analysis needs of your project.

Create collections

Organise your documents into collections. A collection refers to a group of documents that share the same layout or structure. When building a document processing model, it is essential to organise documents into collections based on their layout similarity. This means that for each distinct layout type you want the model to process, you should create a separate collection. For example, if you're building an AI model to process invoices from two different vendors, each with their own unique invoice template, you should create two separate collections – one for each vendor's invoice layout. By organising the invoices into different collections, the model can be trained to handle the distinct differences in layout between the vendors, allowing it to accurately process and extract the necessary information from each type of invoice.

By grouping documents with similar layouts together, the model can better understand the variations in design and more effectively learn the specific patterns and relationships between elements. In practice, the number of collections you create will depend on the diversity of document layouts in your dataset. You can create as many collections as you want. The more varied the layouts, the more collections you will need to ensure the model can handle each unique format effectively. Creating the right number of collections based on layout types is a key step in improving the model's performance and ensuring it can accurately process and extract data from different document styles. The maximum number of collections you can create is 200. All documentation about the requirements (regularly updated) can be found on https://learn.microsoft.com/en-us/ai-builder/form-processing-model-requirements.

In book cataloguing, it may be necessary to create a collection for each type of title page. The AI model will look first at the overall structure of a page and, based on that structure or layout, will interpret the data based on a collection in the model.

What is the definition of a 'type' of title page? How to define a different type? A type of title page refers to a specific arrangement or layout pattern used in the presentation of information on the title page. The type is defined by the structure and sequence in which key elements – such as the title, author name, publisher, date and other details – appear on the page. For example, one type of title page might feature the author's name at the top, followed by the title centred in the middle of the page. Another type might present the title first, followed by a line such as 'written by' and then the author's name. These differences in layout and structure – where information appears on the page and in what order – are what define the 'type' of title page. Each type has a consistent format that can help an AI model recognise and extract information based on expected positions and sequences. This categorisation is essential for processing documents as it allows the model to handle various title page styles effectively by identifying the specific layout type being used.

To train the KBR AI model effectively, we started by scanning a large selection of title pages from books in our collection. After this initial scanning, we organised and categorised these title pages based on their structural differences, allowing us to develop a comprehensive typology of formats. Through this process, we identified around ten distinct types of title page, each characterised by unique layouts and presentation styles. We organised all scans of the same type into individual folders, with each folder containing only title pages that shared the same layout. Then, we created a separate collection for each folder, corresponding to a different title page type. This structure allowed us to streamline the training process by enabling the AI model to learn from distinct collections, each representing a unique layout style. By structuring the data this way, the model could focus on the specific features of each title page type, improving its ability to recognise and accurately process the various layouts in the dataset. This means that when we want to add training data, we need to add images to the right collection. It is important to maintain an organised framework for continuous model training and refinement.

This structured approach significantly enhances the model's ability to extract metadata correctly as it allows it to anticipate and interpret differences in layout. This results in a more efficient and reliable extraction process, especially when dealing with large collections of books with varied title page designs. Figures 3.1–3.3 on the next page show three examples that illustrate the variation in format:

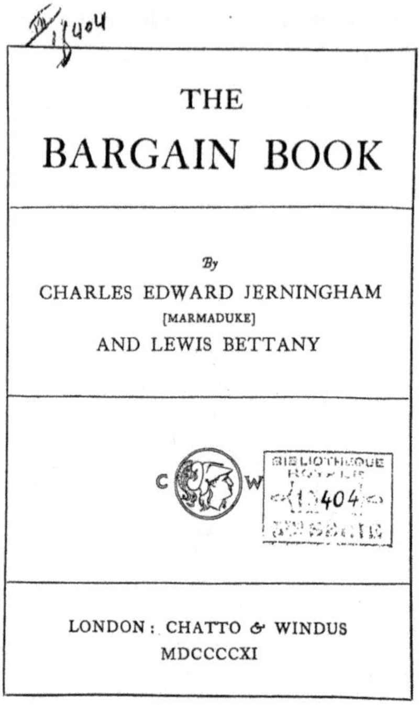

THE

BARGAIN BOOK

By

CHARLES EDWARD JERNINGHAM

[MARMADUKE]

AND LEWIS BETTANY

C W

LONDON: CHATTO & WINDUS

MDCCCCXI

Figure 3.1 *The title appearing first, followed by 'by [Author's Name]'*

L. SECRÉTAN

CHARLES SECRÉTAN

SA VIE ET SON ŒUVRE

LAUSANNE

LIBRAIRIE PAYOT & Cie

1911

Tous droits réservés

Figure 3.2 *The author's name at the top, with the title and publisher information underneath*

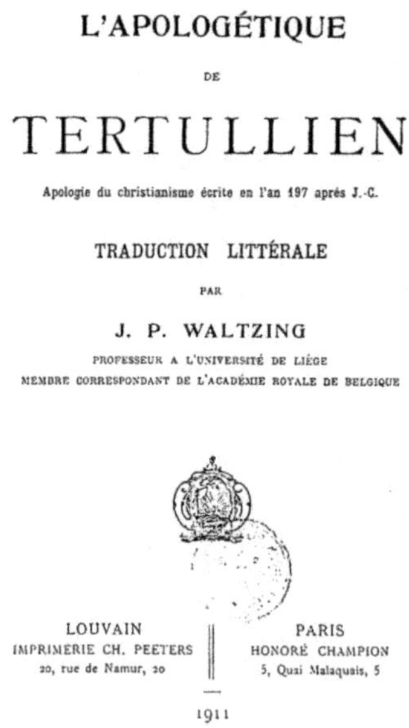

L'APOLOGÉTIQUE

DE

TERTULLIEN

Apologie du christianisme écrite en l'an 197 après J.-C.

TRADUCTION LITTÉRALE

PAR

J. P. WALTZING

PROFESSEUR A L'UNIVERSITÉ DE LIÈGE

MEMBRE CORRESPONDANT DE L'ACADÉMIE ROYALE DE BELGIQUE

LOUVAIN	PARIS
IMPRIMERIE CH. PEETERS	HONORÉ CHAMPION
20, rue de Namur, 20	5, Quai Malaquais, 5

1911

Figure 3.3 *Multiple publishers and/or bookseller listed*

Defining a typology of the title pages is critical to training your model effectively. In one project, for example, we developed a model that recognised tables of contents. Each periodical had a different structure for their table of contents, so each one became its own collection within the model.

Upload your training set

Once you have defined your collections, the next step is to upload your training data. When training an AI Builder model in Power Platform, it is necessary to start with at least five documents per collection. However, to significantly improve the model's accuracy and overall performance, using 10 to 15 documents, or even more, is highly advisable. The more documents you provide, the better the model can learn and adapt to various patterns, improving its ability to recognise and extract the necessary information with greater precision. This additional data helps the model gain a deeper understanding of the content, ensuring that it can handle a wider range of scenarios and deliver more reliable results when deployed. Microsoft also offers documentation on how to improve the model: https://learn.microsoft.com/en-us/ai-builder/improve-form-processing-performance.

Choosing the right training data is crucial. The effectiveness of your model depends on how closely the training data matches the documents it has to process in real-life applications. For example, some title pages may have more creative layouts, with images or uniquely styled text, such as a curvy title. From experience, it is best to train your model using standard title pages with more conventional layouts. Once the model is trained on these, you can then test it on more creatively designed pages to see how well it performs. If you include too many highly creative layouts in your training data, it may negatively impact the accuracy of the results when processing standard title pages, which usually make up the majority. Therefore, for better accuracy, focus on training your model with examples that resemble the majority of the documents it will process.

It is a good practice to keep all the images used for training your model on a separate drive or on your personal computer. This setup allows you to easily add new images whenever you make additional scans or come across a specific title page that you would like to include in the training set. By keeping these training images organised in one location, you can conveniently update the dataset periodically – perhaps every month – by adding new images and retraining the model. Maintaining a separate copy of the images your model is trained on has several organisational benefits. First, it provides a clear reference point for the model's training history, enabling you to track changes in the dataset and understand any adjustments made over time. Second, it allows for easier version control, so you can revert to previous datasets if needed or compare the model's performance before and after new images are added. Lastly, this practice simplifies troubleshooting by allowing you to analyse which images or types of title pages may be affecting the model's accuracy. Overall, maintaining an organised archive of your training images supports the continuous improvement and reliability of the model.

Open data

It can also be highly beneficial to make your training data available as open data. By doing so, other institutions looking to implement similar projects would not need to recreate the entire training set from scratch – scanning title pages, creating typologies and organising images by type. Sharing this data openly could streamline the setup process for future projects, making it easier for institutions to adopt and build on existing work. This approach also opens the door to a collaborative initiative, where different institutions can contribute by uploading images of title pages with unique layouts, creating additional types and collections. By pooling resources in this way, the entire sector could benefit from a richer, more comprehensive dataset, allowing AI models to recognise and classify a wider variety of title page formats. This collaborative model would encourage cross-institutional knowledge-sharing, making it possible to create a robust resource that reflects a diverse range of layouts and styles.

As AI continues to play a larger role in document processing and historical research, the importance of high-quality, diverse training data can't be overstated. Collaboration is essential for developing AI models that can perform well across a variety of document types and formats. By being open about the data that our models are trained on, we promote transparency and reproducibility, which are both cornerstones of open research. Sharing training data as open data supports innovation across institutions and ensures that advancements in AI can benefit the entire community, fostering a culture of openness and accessibility in the development of new technologies. Moreover, it also actively encourages more organisations to explore and adopt AI. By providing a ready-to-use training set, we lower many of the barriers that institutions often face, such as the time, cost and expertise needed to create a dataset from scratch. With access to a comprehensive, well-organised training set, institutions can move past initial hesitations or uncertainties about testing and implementing AI in their workflows. This accessible resource can be a powerful catalyst, making it easier for organisations to experiment with AI, witness its potential firsthand and quickly see the benefits of automated metadata extraction and document processing. Ultimately, this approach boosts confidence in AI, helping institutions take meaningful steps toward digital transformation, improving operational efficiency and fostering a more AI-ready community across sectors.

Later in the book, there is an overview of various document types in which AI can play a significant role in metadata extraction. Each document type presents unique challenges and opportunities for AI-driven metadata extraction and could benefit from such collaborative efforts in creating shared training data.

Tag the documents

Next, tag the important fields in each document. This step involves selecting the text using a mouse and assigning it to the appropriate metadata field (these are the fields you created in the first step 'information to extract'). If a field does not appear on a particular document, mark it as absent. This ensures the model knows how to handle various document formats and missing information.

You can also specify that a particular field is not present across an entire collection. However, it is important to be cautious when doing this. For example, if you indicate that books in a certain collection do not include an edition statement, just because your training set does not have an edition statement and the AI model identifies a new title page as belonging to that collection, it will automatically skip searching for the edition statement, even if it may be present. This is why accurate tagging of documents is a critical task to ensure the AI model correctly identifies and extracts the required information.

Train the model

Once the data is prepared, the model training phase begins. This involves feeding the labelled data into the model, allowing it to learn how to recognise the fields you have tagged across different documents but also patterns and relationships within the documents. The training process may take anywhere from 20 minutes to several hours, depending on the complexity of the documents and the amount of data.

As the model is trained, it is crucial to continuously test its outcomes to evaluate its effectiveness. Testing helps identify whether the model is correctly extracting the information we need, such as names, dates or other relevant details. If the results are unsatisfactory, adjustments must be made. This could involve adding more training data, removing irrelevant or noisy data, restructuring the collections to improve diversity or even redoing the tagging of documents to ensure more precise labelling. The iterative nature of model training means that improvements will be made over time. The model should be regularly tested and refined, with additional rounds of training and validation until the desired accuracy is achieved. As new documents are introduced, the model should be retrained to accommodate these changes and continue improving.

Rename the model

It is also recommended that you rename your model to clearly reflect what it has been trained on. This will make it much easier to identify the purpose and scope of the model at a glance, especially when managing multiple models. A descriptive name helps ensure that you and your team can quickly understand the specific use case or dataset the model is designed for, preventing confusion and improving efficiency in future tasks.

Publish the model

Once the model has been successfully trained, it must be published before it can be utilised in Power Apps or Power Automate workflows. Only published models are available for integration into automated document processing tasks, meaning you will not be able to use the model in any practical applications until this step is completed. Publishing makes the model accessible and ready for real-world use.

Incorporate a feedback loop

One of the critical elements of a well-designed AI-driven system is the ability to continuously improve by incorporating feedback loops. We will focus on how to implement a feedback loop in a Power Automate flow to send images back to the AI model for retraining and why this is crucial for building smarter, more efficient models.

In the context of AI and machine learning, a feedback loop involves the process of continuously collecting new data, analysing it and then using that data to improve the model. In a typical workflow involving AI models for image processing (e.g., object detection or classification), you may want to feed back into the model images that were either incorrectly processed or needed further classification. This retraining process ensures that the AI model becomes more accurate over time, adapting to edge cases and improving its predictive abilities.

In Power Automate, incorporating such a feedback loop means creating a flow that automates the submission of these images back to the AI model, possibly along with user feedback or additional metadata, which can be used to refine the model.

Unfortunately, the validated records in the application do not currently influence the AI model or contribute to its enhancement. Once the model is published, it operates independently. However, Microsoft has recently introduced a feedback loop feature in Power Automate, which allows users to send images back to the model for retraining. This new capability enables the individual responsible for retraining the model to easily incorporate these images as training data. The action in Power Automate to insert this feature is called 'Save File to AI Builder Feedback Loop'.

To determine which images should be sent back to the AI model, we can use the confidence score associated with each field detected by the model. Each field not only provides a value but also includes a confidence score, which ranges from 0 to 1 (or 0% to 100%). For example, if the confidence score is 0.5, it indicates that the model is only 50% certain about the detected field. While a confidence score of 1 signifies complete certainty, it is important to note that, even at this level, the model can still make mistakes. These confidence scores are instrumental in filtering the data. It allows us to focus on information that exceeds a specified confidence threshold while ignoring data that falls below it. For the feedback loop, we can use the confidence levels to identify which images have to be sent back to the model. For example, we might choose to send images where the confidence level for the detected 'Title' is below 0.2. This approach signifies that the model is uncertain about the title in those images, making them prime candidates for retraining. By retraining the model with these less certain cases, we aim to enhance its performance and improve the overall confidence level in future detections. This iterative process can fine-tune the model and ensures that it adapts to new data, ultimately leading to greater accuracy and reliability in its outputs.

After extracting the information, you can add a condition to check the 'Title Confidence Level'. Configure the condition so that if the 'Title Confidence Level' (selected from the dynamic output in the left bar) is set to 'is less than' and the value is entered as 0.2 in the input box to the right, the next step will be triggered. Under the 'If Yes' option, you can add an action to send the image back to the AI Builder feedback loop for further analysis and retraining. That way, if the confidence level is less than 20%, the image will be sent to the AI model for retraining afterwards.

After completing the feedback loop, you can go to your AI model and add images from the 'Feedback Loop' data source to your collection. Once the images are added, you can annotate them, marking the relevant fields or corrections needed and then retrain the model with this updated data. Although this feature is still in preview, it holds great potential for future improvements to the AI model. By continuously feeding the model with challenging cases where its confidence is low, you are actively helping to refine its accuracy and enhance its performance over time. This iterative learning process will enable the model to better handle complex or uncertain data in the future, making it a valuable tool for ongoing model optimisation.

Please note that the feedback loop is currently a preview feature, which means it is still in the early stages of development and may have some limitations. While it offers valuable functionality, such as allowing the model to learn from corrections and improve over time, it may not yet be fully optimised or available for all scenarios. As a preview feature, users might encounter occasional issues or restrictions that could impact performance or usability. It's important to stay informed about updates as the feature is likely to evolve and improve with future releases, offering greater capabilities and fewer limitations. Updates about the feedback loop can be found at: https://learn.microsoft.com/en-us/ai-builder/feedback-loop.

Using the category classification model for subject indexing

Subject indexing is a powerful AI capability that can help to interpret and analyse large volumes of information. After processing images and extracting text, this model allows users to classify content into relevant fields automatically, making it an ideal solution for libraries, document management systems and other data-intensive environments. By applying subject indexing, organisations can enhance data retrieval, improve searchability and optimise classification workflows. This section provides a comprehensive guide to configuring and implementing the subject indexing model, enabling efficient and accurate text classification.

The custom category classification model in AI Builder offers a powerful and versatile solution for organisations looking to create classification systems tailored to their own unique needs. This model can be trained using the specific terms or categories that are most relevant to your operations, whether they involve local jargon, specialised terminology or broader industry classifications. By doing so, the model becomes a seamless extension of your internal or regional classification system, making it perfectly suited to niche or proprietary taxonomies that align with your organisation's distinct requirements. On the other hand, this model can also integrate with globally recognised classification schemes. Whether your organisation needs to adhere to the Universal Decimal Classification (UDC), Dewey Decimal Classification (DDC), Thema, BISAC or other widely accepted standards, the model can be trained to align with these frameworks. This level of adaptability is especially valuable for organisations operating in cross-border contexts or those aiming to standardise their processes according to libraries' best practices.

With its flexibility to handle both custom taxonomies and internationally recognised schemes, the custom category classification model is an invaluable tool for streamlining categorisation, enhancing data organisation and supporting operational consistency across diverse environments. This capability increases efficiency and ensures that your classification system remains relevant and aligned with your specific goals.

Selecting your training data

To get started with setting up and using the custom category classification model, you will need to train it effectively. Carefully selecting and structuring the training data will ensure the model can accurately categorise new information based on the classifications you have defined. Once trained, the model will enhance your ability to organise, retrieve and analyse data according to a structure that truly reflects your requirements, whether they are localised or standardised. This model streamlines the classification process and opens up new possibilities for efficient data management, making it an ideal tool for businesses, libraries and institutions aiming for organised, easily navigable and relevant data categorisation.

Let's take a closer look at the steps involved in building an effective custom category classification model. The first step is to develop a well-prepared training set, which is essential for achieving accurate and reliable results. To do this, begin by setting up a Dataverse table with two main columns: one dedicated to the categories or labels you want to use (such as subject terms or classifications) and the other for the training texts, which can include summaries of books or other relevant textual data. For example, you might populate this table with book summaries from your catalogue, where one column specifies category labels like 'Science Fiction', 'Biography' or 'Philosophy' and the other column includes the corresponding summaries. (The next section covers creating the Dataverse table in more detail.) You can source this data from your organisation's catalogue or by exporting information from other catalogues, such as the Library of Congress (LOC) or https://data.bnf.fr. As long as you have an export that combines texts with their associated subject terms, you have the foundational data needed to train the model effectively.

However, it is crucial to keep in mind that historical data often comes with its own set of challenges. For example, older datasets may contain incorrectly attributed terms, biases embedded within the text or duplicated entries. Such issues can reduce the accuracy of your model if not addressed. Therefore, when working with historical data, it is essential to carefully clean and review the dataset, correcting misattributed terms, removing duplicates and identifying any biases that might skew the model's performance.

Another critical aspect of creating a balanced training set is to maintain an even distribution of terms across your data. For example, if you have 2,000 training entries labelled 'Biology' but only 20 entries labelled 'History', the model may become biased towards biology and less effective at identifying texts that belong in the history category. To avoid this, aim to provide a roughly equal number of training texts for each category. This balance ensures that the model starts interpreting each category from an even foundation, increasing its accuracy and fairness when categorising new texts.

To ensure effective model training, it is also essential to provide at least ten distinct text samples for each tag. This minimum is important – if a tag has fewer than ten examples, the model may not be able to accurately recognise or classify that category, leading to reduced performance and reliability. A lack of sufficient examples can result in the model being unable to capture the nuances or variations within that category, making it harder for the system to make precise predictions. Therefore, it's crucial to gather enough diverse and representative samples for each tag. The more varied and comprehensive the samples are, the better the model can generalise, improving its overall accuracy and effectiveness in classification. By ensuring a solid foundation of training data for every tag, you enable the model to develop a deeper understanding of each category, ultimately leading to better performance and more reliable results.

When setting up your model, you will need to select the language of your training texts. For this reason, it is crucial that the texts in your training data are all in a single, consistent language. Mixing languages within the same dataset can reduce the model's effectiveness as it may lead to inaccuracies in understanding and processing the text. To ensure optimal performance, carefully curate your training data so that every piece of text is in the chosen language. This consistency helps the model better recognise patterns and nuances and thus improves the quality of any predictions or insights generated by the model.

By carefully constructing your training dataset – addressing historical data issues, ensuring term balance, choosing representative texts and in the same language – you will set up your model for success, making it more likely to deliver consistent, unbiased and accurate classifications.

It is possible to assign one, two or even more terms to a single text. To do this, you can list multiple terms in the same column, separating them with a semicolon or another chosen delimiter. Later, we will see how you can specify this delimiter within the model settings to allow the system to recognise and interpret each term individually. This setup enables the model to associate a single text with multiple categories or topics, making it especially useful for nuanced or multifaceted texts that span several subjects.

Creating the Dataverse table

To train a category classification AI model, you will need to set up a Dataverse table as this is the required format for connecting and training the model within Power Platform. However, it is helpful to start by preparing and refining your training data in an Excel file. Working in Excel gives you flexibility: you can easily add new rows, remove duplicates, filter data and make other adjustments to ensure the data is clean and accurate. This simplifies data management, making it easy to prepare, validate and structure your data. Once you have organised your training data in Excel and are confident of its quality, you can create a Dataverse table directly from the Excel file.

Creating a Dataverse table from an Excel file is a straightforward process, thanks to built-in features that allow you to import and convert data into a Dataverse table. First, ensure that your data is well-organised. Each column should have a clear header and each row should represent a distinct record. Avoid any blank rows or columns as these can cause issues during import. Dataverse typically supports '.xlsx' files, so save your file in this format if it is not already. Once in Power Apps, from the left-hand navigation pane, select 'Tables'. Select 'Import' – 'Import Data'. You also have the option to choose 'Import Data from Excel', which allows you to directly bring in data from your Excel file into Dataverse. However, if you select the 'Import Data' option, you will be guided through a more detailed, step-by-step approach to the import process. Drag your file into the upload box or choose data source Excel workbook and upload the file. Click 'Next' and select the workbook with your data (if your Excel has multiple workbooks). Click 'Next' and select how you want to load the data: to a new table or to an existing table. Dataverse may automatically detect and map some of the columns based on the headers in your Excel file. You will need to review these mappings to ensure each column in Excel corresponds to the correct field type in Dataverse (e.g., Text, Number, Date). If you load to an existing table you can choose to append the data to the existing data. This can be useful if you want to add other training data to an existing Dataverse. You can also 'merge' with existing records. If necessary, you can adjust field names, data types and other settings to match Dataverse's data structure. After configuring the table and mappings, review the summary screen to ensure everything looks correct and start the import and publication phase. Your Dataverse table is now ready to be used in an AI category classification model.

Training the model

Setting up the category classification model begins by selecting your Dataverse table followed by selecting the column that contains the texts or summaries you wish to analyse. Next, select the column that contains the 'tags' (terms or categories) associated with those texts. If a text has multiple tags, you can choose the used separator for this column, such as a semicolon, comma or tab. Next, review your data to ensure everything is properly formatted and accurate. Then you can select the language of your text samples. Currently, the model supports English, German, French, Italian, Portuguese and Spanish. This means that the training data must be provided in one of these languages for optimal performance.

For organisations handling multilingual content, such as at KBR where we operate in a trilingual country with Dutch, French and German as official languages, this language limitation could present some obstacles. In addition, libraries and institutions often hold materials published in a wide variety of languages, reflecting the cultural and linguistic diversity of their collections. If your institution works with languages outside the supported set, these limitations may require additional resources or workarounds. One very practical workaround is using Power Automate to translate your text into a supported language. For example, if you are working with texts in Dutch but your model is trained only on English data, you can start by using Power Automate to translate the Dutch text into English. Once translated, you can send the English text to the model in the next step. This way, the model can process it and apply the appropriate category classification, allowing you to make use of the model even when the original texts are in a different language. We will come back to this procedure later. If you are working with highly linguistically diverse materials, we recommend using GPT (Generative Pre-trained Transformer) prompts. One of the key advantages of prompts is their ability to interpret and process multiple languages seamlessly, without requiring you to specify the language beforehand or translate the text. We will explore this aspect of prompts in more detail later.

Things to keep in mind when using the category classification model

Limit of 200 tags

In Microsoft's category classification model, you have the flexibility to train up to 200 unique tags. Each tag represents a category that the model will identify and extract from the given text. However, there may be situations where 200 tags will not be sufficient, particularly if you are using the model in a library context for comprehensive classification or subject indexing. Libraries often deal with vast and diverse collections that cover a wide range of topics and this requires a far greater level of specificity to accurately reflect the nuances within various subjects and genres.

Some well-known classification schemes, such as DDC, UDC and Thema, are structured hierarchically. In these systems, you start with a set of broad, general categories – typically ten or more. From there, each main category branches out into increasingly specific subcategories, resembling a tree structure, also known as an arborescent or hierarchical model. This hierarchical structure allows for a detailed and organised breakdown of topics, helping users navigate from broad concepts to very specific subjects. Recent research into automated classification has indicated that implementing a hierarchical approach might improve the accuracy and effectiveness of classification systems. Testing how hierarchical models perform in an automated context could lead to more refined and accurate categorisation, enhancing both the precision of classification and the ease of retrieving relevant information. However, this is not without issues:

> Since DDC is highly hierarchical, its built-in relationships could help with disambiguation, especially in lexical algorithms. However, Annif backends do not currently support hierarchical classification so this should be experimented in the future.
>
> (Golub et al., 2024, 1077)

We tried to solve this issue by creating a hierarchical system of automatic classification. Taking the example of DDC or UDC: we have one model that first trains the general category: 000, 100, 200, 300, etc. Then, for each of those general categories, we have another model trained to attribute a more specific classification, for example, one that can attribute a more specific term. For example, a paper by Snežana Stojiljković (1998) has the following summary/abstract:

> The cognitive-developmental approach to morality represents a wider theoretical framework of this research. The study had as its objective to determine the relative contribution of some personality characteristics to moral judgement at different developmental levels. More precisely, moral judgement is connected with an individual's intellectual abilities, empathy and Eysenck's basic dimensions of personality.
>
> (Stojiljkovi, 1998, 507)

In our automated classification system and based on this summary, the first model would identify the general UDC code '1 Philosophy. Psychology'. Once this broad category is detected, a second, specialised model is triggered to refine the classification further. This second model is specifically trained to recognise and classify terms within the broader '1 Philosophy. Psychology' category, so it can differentiate more precisely among subcategories such as '101', '11', '111', '113', '122-129', '12', '13', '14' and other related codes. With this multi-level approach, there's even an option to add a third layer of classification for increased specificity. For example, the first model may determine that the item generally fits under '1 Philosophy. Psychology'. The second model then narrows it down to a specific area, such as '159.9 Psychology'. Finally, a third model, trained only with subcategories within '159.9 Psychology', might classify it further into '159.923 Psychology of Personality'. This hierarchical classification system enables a precise, multi-layered method for categorising complex content. It offers a broad overview while also drilling down into progressively detailed areas, facilitating easier organisation and more detailed indexing.

Level of maintenance

Regular updates to the training set and retraining the model are necessary to keep the classification accurate, especially as new categories or texts are added. You can update your model by adding new data to your Dataverse table through an Excel import. Once the new data is successfully uploaded, simply click the 'retrain' button in the model to refresh its learning. This process ensures that your model stays up to date with the latest information, allowing it to improve its performance over time. By regularly adding new data and retraining the model, you help it adapt to evolving trends or patterns, ultimately increasing its accuracy and relevance in handling future tasks.

Understanding the model's output

Understanding why a model makes specific decisions can be difficult, particularly when it misclassifies certain texts. These misclassifications can often seem mysterious or unpredictable. This is especially the case with complex models that operate as 'black boxes', making it hard to see how and why they arrived at a given conclusion. A 'black box' in the context of technology and machine learning refers to a system or model whose internal workings are not visible or understandable to the user. You can see the input and output, but the process by which the system arrives at a particular result is hidden or too complex to interpret easily. This lack of transparency can be problematic, especially in fields like healthcare or legal, where understanding the 'why' behind a decision is as important as the decision itself. Identifying and addressing these errors is essential to improving a model's performance as each mistake can highlight weaknesses or gaps in the training data.

However, the process of monitoring the model's decisions, spotting errors and then refining the training set accordingly can be incredibly time-consuming, especially when dealing with datasets containing thousands or even tens of thousands of texts.

Regularly reviewing and fine-tuning the dataset is crucial for refining the model's accuracy. This task demands significant time and resources as every update requires careful analysis and judgement. Despite the challenges, investing time in manually adjusting the training set can help ensure that the model learns from its mistakes, gradually reducing error rates and leading to a more reliable, accurate system over time. This ongoing cycle of monitoring, error correction and refinement is what ultimately transforms a good model into a highly effective one.

Biases in the training set

The quality and consistency of the training data are paramount. For example, at KBR, we initially used data from existing records (summaries and subject terms). This data is historical and compiled by different cataloguers and publishers over time, introducing variability and potential biases. A better approach might be to create a training set from a smaller, more controlled dataset. This way, you can ensure uniformity in the language and terminology used, resulting in a more reliable model.

Category classification model for subject indexing: conclusion

Despite the considerations mentioned above, using Microsoft's category classification model is an effective way to approach subject indexing.

As this book is centred around Microsoft's Power Platform, and because we have ready access to Microsoft's category classification model within this ecosystem, it is recommended that you start with this model as your primary indexing tool. The Power Platform provides an integrated, streamlined experience that can simplify the process of categorising and managing content, making it an ideal starting point for most users. We will explain how to incorporate subject indexing in a Power Automate flow in Chapter 4.

However, this method is not the only possibility to tackle subject indexing. Other tools, like the open-source tool Annif and large language models (LLMs), such as OpenAI's ChatGPT, can also be used to categorise and index content. Various institutions have explored multiple options for subject indexing, each with its own strengths and weaknesses depending on the specific goals and technological environment in place (Salaba and Saccucci, 2021). We will show later how to interact with these tools through their APIs, allowing you to explore additional indexing methods and enrich your projects with a broader range of classification capabilities. However, the use of LLMs has become much easier since 2024, with the introduction of GPT Prompts in the AI Builder within the Power Platform. This integration allows users to leverage the power of LLMs directly within Power Automate, eliminating the need for API configurations and making advanced text classification and automation more accessible than ever.

Using a GPT-based prompt for subject indexing

A new feature in the Power Platform is the integration of GPT, enabling users to leverage advanced AI capabilities through the use of prompts. This enhancement offers the significant advantage of working with an LLM trained on billions of text samples, allowing it to interpret, analyse and generate text with exceptional accuracy and nuance. Moreover, there is no need to restrict this tool to a single language. The GPT model is capable of automatically detecting and working with multiple languages, allowing for greater flexibility and versatility in diverse linguistic environments. This makes it particularly beneficial for users operating in multilingual settings or those handling content in various languages.

One of the standout aspects of this feature is the ability to tailor the prompt to your specific classification scheme. For example, this can be by creating a variable containing your own 'input categories'. Additionally, you have the option to connect this functionality to a table in Dataverse so that you can store all your (local) classification or subject terms. Microsoft provides some standard prompts as an example, but you can customise it further to suit your unique requirements. For example, you can specify as a prompt:

> Classify the [Input text] into one of the [input categories].

Or

> Classify the [Input text] into one of the [Classification.ColumnTerms].

In the second example, 'Classification' refers to a table and 'ColumnTerms' represents the name of the column containing the desired terms that the prompt will use for classification. This approach enables precise and dynamic categorisation based on the specific data provided in your table. In other words, when using this feature within Power Automate, you have the flexibility to define your own classifications and maintain that list easily.

We would recommend to not only make a list of the classifications, but also add contextual information about a term, allowing the prompt to incorporate that information into its analysis. For example, a list of categories could include:

Geography
Archeology
Prehistory

However, a more effective approach would be to structure the list in a way that clearly separates the category name from its contextual description. This can be done by placing a semicolon between the two parts. The portion before the semicolon should serve as the actual output value, while the text following it provides additional context or clarification:

Geography; Geography studies the Earth's physical features and human-environment interactions. It includes topics like cartography, climate and urban development. Geography provides tools for sustainable planning and resource management.
Archeology; Archeology examines material remains to understand past civilisations. It includes artifacts, structures, and landscapes. This field bridges history and science to reconstruct human stories.
Prehistory and ancient history; This field studies human history before written records and early civilisations. It includes topics like early human development and ancient societies. These studies reveal the foundations of human culture.

By modifying this contextual text, you can influence and enhance the outcome of the prompt. This feature provides tremendous potential for subject indexing, primarily because it allows you to restrict responses to local terms, ensuring that the outputs are limited to precisely what you need. By tailoring the classification to your specific terminology, you maintain control over the results, aligning them closely with your organisational or project requirements.

The seamless integration of this functionality into Power Automate flows also enhances its practicality and efficiency (see Chapter 5). Another significant benefit is the flexibility a prompt provides. With carefully crafted prompting, you can achieve the exact outcome you desire. For example, you can request the system to explain its choice of classification. This allows you to understand the reasoning behind a particular result, which can be invaluable for refining the prompt or assessing whether additional context should be included. Such explanations can also help identify any gaps or ambiguities in the provided context. By analysing the outcome and the explanation, you gain insights into how the system interprets your input, enabling you to adjust the prompt to make it more precise or relevant. This iterative process not only enhances the accuracy of the results but also helps streamline the classification workflow by ensuring clarity and alignment between the prompt and the data source. This combination of customisation, workflow integration and adaptability makes the feature a powerful tool for library cataloguing, where precision and adaptability are critical.

While using prompts for subject indexing offers potential, there are also some disadvantages and risks to consider, even when the classifications are local. One potential issue is a lack of consistency in the results as the model may interpret prompts differently depending on phrasing or context. This variability can lead to discrepancies in classification, making it difficult to ensure uniformity across indexed content. Additionally, relying on prompts might result in the omission of relevant terms or concepts if the prompt is not sufficiently detailed. If the classification is overly specific or lacks sufficient context, the model may struggle to accurately capture the full range of meanings or nuances. This is why it is important to add context to each term. Moreover, the absence of human oversight or insight into the data the model is trained on can increase the risk of incorrect or biased indexing, especially if the model misinterprets subtle contextual differences.

In summary, working with prompts is a dynamic and powerful approach that can be fine-tuned to deliver specific, well-reasoned outputs while providing opportunities for continuous improvement. This tool opens up a wide range of possibilities for incorporating GPT into your cataloguing and subject indexing workflows, but the output always has to be handled with caution.

Entity extraction and key phrase extraction

Unlike the category classification model, entity extraction and key phrase extraction are not designed to assign new information to a term or interpret the meaning of the text. Instead, their primary function is to extract entities or key phrases directly from the content. This means that the output consists solely of information that is explicitly stated in the text itself, without any added contextualisation or inferred meanings. For example, if the text mentions 'John bought three apples from the market in London', the application would extract entities like 'John' as person name, 'London' as city and key phrases such as 'bought three apples'. However, it would not interpret or categorise this information further. This straightforward approach makes these applications particularly useful for scenarios where precise and unbiased extraction of information is critical. They can play a vital role in enhancing the organisation, retrieval and analysis of resources. Some specific use cases are outlined below.

Entity extraction

Entity extraction can automatically identify key details such as author names, publication dates, publishers and geographic locations from the text of books, articles or manuscripts. These entities can then populate metadata fields in the library catalogue, reducing manual effort and improving accuracy.

Extracting entities from sources such as summaries, back cover text or other text fragments can play a vital role in enhancing bibliographic descriptions. These entities can be used to add subject access fields, which, in the MARC21 format, are typically found in the 6XX fields. By identifying key topics, themes or subjects from these textual elements, cataloguers can create richer, more accurate subject headings that improve discoverability and relevance for library users. For example, in a book about Leonard Cohen, the back cover text mentioned that 'Leonard Cohen lived in Montréal'. If we use this sentence in the 'quick test' of the entity extraction model this is the result:

Leonard Cohen	PersonName
Montréal	City

Once the relevant entities have been extracted from a given text, they can be used to significantly enhance bibliographic records. (We will see how this can be achieved using Power Automate later in the book.) This is where the true value of entity extraction comes into play – it allows us to enrich the metadata in meaningful ways. For example, when we extract a person's name, like 'Leonard Cohen', we can integrate this information into the bibliographic description. In MARC21, this would be placed in field 600 (Subject Added Entry – Personal Name), which is dedicated to adding personal names as subject headings. Alternatively, in BIBFRAME, we can map it to the element 'bf:subject/bf:agent/bf:person', which serves a similar purpose within the BIBFRAME framework. By doing so, we make the record more precise and searchable, improving its discoverability in databases and catalogues.

Similarly, if we extract a city name, like 'Montréal', we can enrich the record by including it in field 651 (Subject Added Entry – Geographic Name) in MARC21, which is specifically used for geographic terms related to the content. In BIBFRAME, this information would be added to the element 'bf:subject/bf:place', which captures the geographic subject of the resource. Adding this type of information enhances the record's metadata, allowing it to be more easily identified and categorised in various contexts, such as location-based searches. These enhancements improve the accuracy and completeness of bibliographic records and ensure that the records are more useful to users searching for specific authors or locations, making the cataloguing process more efficient and comprehensive.

Once the entities are extracted, they can be further enriched by linking them to external resources, which adds an additional layer of value to the bibliographic record. For example, using the geographic name 'Montréal' in your Power Automate flow, you can easily incorporate an HTTP search that connects to a comprehensive geographical database, like GeoNames. By querying this resource, you can retrieve much more than just the name of a location. For example, from the search results, you can extract a unique identifier for the geographic name, ensuring that the information you have is accurate and linked to a globally recognised reference system. This identifier can be invaluable as it enables the record to be connected to other systems and resources across the world, enhancing the consistency and interoperability of the data. But the benefits do not stop there. By using GeoNames or similar databases, you can access a wide range of additional geographic details. These might include exact co-ordinates (latitude and longitude) or administrative levels (such as the city, province or country). All these details can then be seamlessly integrated into your bibliographic record, making it much more comprehensive. Instead of a simple name, your record will contain precise, verifiable information, which enhances both its usability and its value to researchers and users who rely on accurate geographic data. This approach improves the quality of your records, makes them richer and more connected to the global web of (geographic) knowledge. It makes the resource more discoverable and informative, providing users with richer context when searching for specific locations. This is particularly valuable for researchers, librarians and information professionals who rely on precise, well-structured data. In the next chapter, we will delve deeper into how you can incorporate external resources like GeoNames to further enrich bibliographic records in your Power Automate flow.

Extracting entities from the copyright page of a publication can help identify all contributors, such as authors, editors, illustrators or translators. By associating each contributor with their specific role, this information can be used to populate added entry fields in the bibliographic record. In MARC21, these details are recorded in the 7XX fields. Including this level of detail acknowledges the contributions of individuals involved in the creation of a work and facilitates more precise and comprehensive bibliographic records. This, in turn, aids users in finding materials that match their specific needs or interests.

By leveraging entity extraction methods effectively, libraries can significantly improve the quality and functionality of their cataloguing systems, ensuring a richer and more user-friendly experience for patrons.

Key phrase extraction

Key phrase extraction can be used to generate concise summaries or abstracts for books, articles or research papers by identifying and pulling out the most relevant phrases and concepts. This approach allows users to quickly assess the relevance and value of a resource, enabling them to make informed decisions about whether to engage with the content more deeply. By automatically highlighting key ideas and themes, it provides an efficient way to capture the essence of a resource in just a few words or sentences. Key phrase extraction can be instrumental in helping a cataloguer add appropriate subject terms and keywords to the bibliographic record. This process ensures that the record accurately reflects the content of the resource and enhances its discoverability in catalogue searches. However, we can take this even further by exploring how key phrase extraction could support automated subject indexing, not just based on a concise summary of the content or the back cover text, but on key phrases drawn from the entire text. This holistic approach would result in more accurate and nuanced indexing, capturing subtle themes and concepts that might be overlooked if we relied solely on summary-level key phrases.

For example, if a cataloguer were to extract key phrases from the full text of an academic paper, they could identify key concepts, recurring themes and pivotal arguments that are central to the work's content. This information could then be used to create more detailed subject headings and keywords, enabling users to find resources based on the depth and complexity of the original text. By doing so, we ensure that academic cataloguing and indexing reflect the nuances of scholarly work, supporting a more sophisticated and contextually rich approach to resource discovery and retrieval.

In summary, combining entity and key phrase extraction can help transform unstructured text into structured, machine-readable data. These processes allow you to identify and pull out important information like names, dates, locations and significant terms from any text, such as a book summary or back cover description. By using the prebuilt models available in Power Platform, you can automatically extract relevant data without manual attribution. This capability provides additional layers of information. It enables the conversion of entities, making them searchable and useful for a wide range of applications. Since this process is fully automated and requires no additional time or effort from cataloguers, it becomes possible to add these extra layers of information seamlessly. In this way, automation streamlines the workflow but also enhances bibliographic records by integrating valuable data that would be difficult or time-consuming to gather manually. It adds meaningful information that might otherwise be overlooked, ensuring that bibliographic records are more comprehensive and useful for researchers, librarians, publishers and anyone working with large volumes of text as it improves the way data is catalogued, searched and retrieved.

Inclusive metadata creation

Using AI tools integrated into Power Platform can significantly enhance inclusivity in bibliographic records, particularly through robust language support. These tools are capable of recognising and detecting various languages and scripts through text recognition features, making bibliographic records more accessible to a wider and more diverse audience.

Once a language is detected, you can use AI-powered translation models to translate the content into your preferred language. This capability ensures that translations can be easily provided in the language of your users and patrons, allowing them to engage with and understand the material. By incorporating these translations, the accessibility of records is expanded and they become useful for multilingual communities.

In addition to language translation, AI can play a vital role in enriching subject indexing models by automatically identifying and adding relevant text. This deepens the level of detail within the bibliographic records and improves their discoverability, making it easier for users to find and access relevant information.

In the above section of the book covering the document processing model, as well as in the section focusing on subject indexing, we discussed the importance of collaboration. There are important potential benefits in libraries, museums and all cultural heritage institutions taking a collaborative approach. It allows these institutions to work together more effectively in the creation of shared training data. In Chapter 1, we explored the concept of inclusivity. A collaborative approach is key to building a truly global and inclusive cataloguing system. Instead of limiting the training set to reflect the perspective of a single library, country or culture, we can take a more expansive approach. By fostering collaboration among multiple institutions and pooling resources, we can create a more comprehensive and diverse training set that leads to bibliographic records that are inclusive of various cultural perspectives, languages, traditions and historical contexts. This makes bibliographic systems more accessible and ensures they are representative of the vast diversity of human knowledge and culture.

I presented this idea at the IFLA Satellite Meeting in 2023 in Brussels (Lowagie, 2023b), proposing that institutions should join forces to create such a comprehensive and inclusive training set. By working together, libraries, museums and other cultural heritage institutions can make significant strides toward developing more equitable and globally relevant cataloguing systems, ultimately contributing to a more inclusive and interconnected world of knowledge. This type of collaboration offers significant benefits beyond simply improving the quality of bibliographic records. By bringing together various institutions and perspectives, it can also play a vital role in promoting cultural diversity and inclusivity in how knowledge is categorised and accessed. When libraries, museums and cultural heritage organisations collaborate, they bring together a wide range of expertise, traditions and viewpoints, which can enrich the way we organise and interpret information. This collaborative approach ensures that diverse cultural perspectives are not overlooked and it fosters a more holistic view of the world's knowledge. It helps avoid the biases that can arise when only one group or culture is represented, allowing for a richer and more balanced representation of ideas. Additionally, by including materials from different cultures and regions, these efforts make knowledge more accessible and relevant to a global audience, empowering individuals from all backgrounds to engage with information in ways that resonate with their own cultural contexts. Ultimately, collaboration across institutions can pave the way for a more inclusive, global system of knowledge organisation that reflects the true breadth of human experience and intellectual achievement. This inclusive approach benefits not just researchers or academics, but anyone seeking to explore the vast world of information and culture.

CHAPTER 4

Building the Cataloguing Application

Planning the application

When planning a cataloguing app, it is essential to consider several key factors to ensure the app is both user-friendly and effective in fulfilling its intended purpose. One of the most crucial elements in developing an application is designing the user interface (UI) as it fundamentally influences how cataloguers and users interact with the app. The UI serves as the bridge between the user and the functionality of the application, shaping the overall experience. The design of the interface is not arbitrary but is closely guided by the specific purpose of the application and the workflow it is intended to facilitate. For example, if the app is aimed at cataloguing large volumes of data, the UI must prioritise efficiency and clarity, offering tools like streamlined navigation, intuitive input methods and robust search functionalities. By aligning the UI design with the app's goals and the workflow of its users, developers can create an intuitive, effective and enjoyable user experience that ensures the application meets its objectives.

This chapter will provide an overview of the key questions you need to consider and will walk you through the process of implementing the core features of an application. While the chapter will guide you in building a single example application, the primary goal is not just to create one specific app but to help you deeply understand how all the features function. This knowledge is essential because the example application may not fully meet the specific needs of your organisation. Instead, the focus is on equipping you with the insights and skills to adapt and customise these features to suit your unique requirements.

To ensure you gain a well-rounded perspective, this chapter will also explore various possibilities and alternative approaches for implementing features, giving you the flexibility to design an application that aligns perfectly with your goals. By the end of the chapter, you will have a practical example but also the foundational knowledge to confidently tailor the app to your organisation's needs.

Before you begin, it is crucial to ask: *What is the primary purpose of this app?* Clearly defining the app's main objectives will guide your design decisions and the functionality you need to include. Here are some important questions to help clarify the app's role:

- Will the app be used for validating metadata? If the app is meant to validate metadata, it will need a user-friendly interface that allows cataloguers to review, edit and approve records efficiently. A search interface and gallery view can help users quickly locate the records they need to validate. Additionally, consider adding validation rules or alerts to flag inconsistencies, ensuring that the metadata remains accurate and reliable.
- Is the goal to complete a full bibliographic record or just a basic record to be further developed in your LMS? If the app is intended to create only a basic bibliographic record, a simplified interface might be sufficient. However, if your goal is to complete detailed records, you will need to provide more advanced functionalities, such as fields for complex metadata input, validation mechanisms and perhaps even options for linking to external databases or records for enhanced accuracy.
- Is the app intended to capture scans of documents or physical items? One of the key features is the ability to scan documents. You have a few options for how to implement this. For example, using camera control within Power Apps, you can allow users to take photos directly within the app. These images can then be sent to an AI model for processing, helping to automate the cataloguing process. Alternatively, you could integrate a form processor or use an external application.
- Will the app be used to attribute tasks and divide work among cataloguers? If the app's primary function is task distribution, you should incorporate features that enable collaborative work. This could include dashboards to visualise task progress, workflows for assigning and tracking tasks and user management tools to ensure smooth co-operation among cataloguers. These features will streamline the division of labour and enhance the efficiency of your cataloguing team.
- Where will you save the data? Another important consideration is where you will store the data captured and processed by your app. You can immediately create a file containing the metadata, such as a MARC21XML, or save your data in a Dataverse table or in an Excel file. The choice of storage will impact how data is accessed and managed, but also the security, scalability and long-term maintenance of the

cataloguing records. Be sure to select a storage solution that aligns with your organisation's requirements.

Designing a cataloguing app involves creating a functional and intuitive tool that enhances the workflow for cataloguers while ensuring that records are accurate and comprehensive. By asking (and answering) the right questions and considering key factors, you can design an app that meets the needs of your users.

Designing the user interface

Designing a user-friendly and efficient UI is critical to meeting the cataloguing needs of librarians. A well-crafted UI ensures that tasks such as entering metadata, searching for catalogued records and managing collections are performed smoothly and with minimal friction. The goal is to create a system that is both easy to use and highly functional, accommodating the different needs of its diverse user base. Below are some key considerations and tips for achieving an optimal UI design.

Simplicity

The primary consideration when designing a cataloguing UI is simplicity. The interface should be intuitive and easy to navigate. Complex menus, unnecessary steps or cluttered designs can overwhelm users, leading to inefficiencies and frustration. The layout should be straightforward, with clearly labelled sections and logical workflows. Consistent placement of buttons, tabs and search fields ensures that users can quickly familiarise themselves with the system. For example, placing the search bar prominently at the top of the screen allows easy access to one of the most frequently used functions. For a bilingual institution like KBR, it is essential that we provide labels in both French and Dutch to ensure that all users can navigate the system with ease. Offering multilingual support allows users to interact with the platform in their preferred language.

The standard buttons and input fields provided by Power Apps, such as text fields, drop-down menus, combo boxes, date pickers and checkboxes, are highly intuitive and user-friendly. However, you have the flexibility to customise their appearance, including adjusting the style, colour, background colour, hover colour and hover fill colour, among other options.

To streamline the design process, you can create a single example of each button or input field with your preferred settings and then reuse these elements for other functionalities. This approach saves time by preventing the need to manually adjust the parameters for each new button or input field as they would otherwise default to the standard Power Apps blue styling. By duplicating your customised elements, you maintain a consistent look and feel across the app, enhancing both usability and visual cohesion. Changing colours in Power Apps is a simple process. To do this, select the parameter you want to modify – such as HoverColor – from the drop-down options list located above the element. Once you've chosen the parameter, there are two options for specifying the colour. You can either enter an RGBA code, such as 'RGBA(0, 0, 0, 1)' for black, where the values represent red, green, blue and the alpha (transparency) channel, or you can type in a predefined colour by using the Color. function. For example, you could type 'Color.Red' for red or 'Color.White' for white. This flexibility allows you to either define exact colour values using RGBA or quickly choose from preset colours, making customisation both precise and convenient.

Metadata entry

Metadata entry is a core part of any cataloguing system. The input forms designed for this purpose should be simple yet comprehensive, allowing users to modify the extracted metadata. This could include editable fields for titles, authors, publication dates, ISBNs, subject categories and more. Providing clear guidance for each field – perhaps through 'Hint text' (the text shown in the input field as a hint) – helps reduce errors and speeds up the data entry process. Drop-down menus can help to further enhance efficiency and accuracy (particularly for standardised fields with fixed possibilities, such as language or country). The layout should be logical, presenting related fields together and minimising scrolling by avoiding overly long forms.

Search functionality

The search functionality within a cataloguing system must be powerful, yet easy to use. Users should be able to quickly retrieve specific records or browse through collections without difficulty. Incorporating filters such as author, genre, publication year or language allows for more refined searches, catering to the diverse needs of users. It is also essential to ensure that search results are presented in a user-friendly way, with sortable columns and easy-to-read summaries of each catalogued record.

Intuitive design

One of the most important tips for designing a cataloguing UI is to ensure that it is intuitive. Every action should be self-explanatory, with minimal instruction needed. Organise workflows in such a way that users can accomplish tasks, such as cataloguing new materials or searching for records, in the least number of steps possible. For example, when cataloguing new items, provide clear and logical steps that guide the user through the process without unnecessary clicks or distractions. Icons, buttons and navigation menus should be easily recognisable, helping users quickly understand what actions are available to them. Streamlining workflows is essential for efficiency, particularly in cataloguing where the repetition of tasks is common. Reducing the number of steps required to complete routine actions can save users significant time and effort.

Feedback mechanisms

A UI is never static – there's always room for improvement. By incorporating user feedback mechanisms you can gather valuable insights from librarians and end-users to continuously refine the interface. This could be in the form of a feedback button directly in the UI, allowing users to report issues or suggest improvements in real time. Alternatively, periodic surveys or usability testing sessions can offer deeper insights into pain points and areas for enhancement. Actively seeking and implementing feedback demonstrates a commitment to user satisfaction and system improvement.

In conclusion, designing a UI for a cataloguing app involves balancing simplicity with functionality, ensuring that all user needs are addressed. By focusing on ease of navigation, efficient metadata entry, robust search capabilities and accessibility, while also keeping the design intuitive and open to user feedback, you can create a highly effective interface. A well-designed UI makes the cataloguing process more efficient and enhances the overall experience for both librarians and end-users.

Designing the key features

This section provides an overview of the various options available for the key features of the app, specifically in relation to the questions raised earlier regarding the app's main objectives. By exploring these options, we can better understand how the app's core functionality aligns with its intended purpose, ensuring that the design and features effectively meet user needs. This analysis also helps in identifying the most suitable approaches for implementing these features.

Scanning or uploading images

One of the main features of a cataloguing app might involve scanning documents or items to add to the bibliographic record. There are several ways you can approach this, depending on the tools integrated into the app.

Using camera control in Power Apps

Power Apps offers built-in camera control, allowing users to take photos directly within the app. If you want to take photos in the app, the design should incorporate a smooth process for taking and uploading images using a device's camera. Be aware that photos taken in Power Apps have a lower resolution than the camera of your mobile phone. Images generated by the camera control have a maximum resolution of 640 x 480 pixels. Another important factor to consider is the availability of automatic border detection in some applications, which allows users to scan only the specific page they intend to capture, excluding any surrounding elements. This feature ensures that the scanned image is clean and focused solely on the relevant content. This can greatly improve the accuracy of subsequent data analysis. Unfortunately, Power Apps does not yet support automatic border detection.

Once the photos are captured, they can be sent to a workflow (flow) for further processing by an AI model. This AI model can extract relevant metadata or text from the image, helping to automate the cataloguing process.

Using the form processor in Power Apps

Another powerful tool for handling document scans is the Form Processor feature. To implement this, follow these steps:

1. Click on 'Insert' in Power Apps, then select 'AI Builder' and choose 'Form Processor'.
2. Once the form processor is in place, select a published Document Processing AI model of your environment. This will be the model that will interpret the image.
3. Click the 'Analyze' button to add an image. If using a PC, the user can upload an image from their device. On a mobile device, users have the additional option to choose an image from their photo library or use the camera to take a scan directly within the app.
4. After the image is uploaded or captured, the AI model will then analyse the image and extract the relevant data based on the AI model's configuration. The extracted information can be integrated into the bibliographic record or used to populate fields automatically, saving cataloguers a significant amount of time.

The analysis process can sometimes take a while, which may slow down the overall workflow. After each photo is taken, you must wait for the analysis to be completed before moving on. This is one of the main reasons why KBR decided not to use the Form Processor feature. The need to pause and wait after every scan can hinder productivity, especially in scenarios where quick processing is essential for efficient cataloguing or data entry. As a result, KBR opted for alternative solutions that allow for a smoother, more streamlined workflow.

Using an external application

For the KBR retrocataloguing project, it was crucial that scanning could be done offline since internet coverage (particularly Wi-Fi) in the stacks is limited. To address this, we decided to separate the scanning process from the validation step. Our workflow involved using a book scanner connected to a laptop to scan the books directly in the stacks. Once the scans were completed, we would upload the images to SharePoint. As soon as a file was added to SharePoint, a Power Automate flow was triggered, initiating the processing and AI analysis of the images and saving the data in Dataverse, showing the data in the Power App.

In another project, focused on automating the scanning of contemporary books, we opted for a different approach and used mobile phones for document scanning via OneDrive or Microsoft Lens. These applications include a document scanning feature with automatic border detection, making the process smoother and more efficient. This feature can be quite valuable, especially when working with AI models that process scanned images. A clear, high-quality scan, where only the page intended for analysis is captured, can significantly enhance the results. Reducing visual noise from extraneous elements in the scan allows the AI to better focus on the text or data that needs to be extracted, leading to more reliable and accurate outcomes. Additionally, these scanning apps allow users to upload images directly to OneDrive or SharePoint, triggering a Power Automate flow and integrating the images in your Power Platform environment and Power App. We favoured this option because it offers greater flexibility in how scans are taken. Scanning can be done offline and the work divided among different people, making the overall workflow more efficient. However, a drawback of this approach is that it requires the use of two separate applications, meaning the entire process isn't fully integrated into a single system. While this dual-application workflow introduces some complexity, the flexibility, the document scanning features and the potential for labour division make it a practical solution in certain contexts.

Create files or saving data

When it comes to creating or saving extracted data, there are several approaches you can take, depending on your specific needs and workflow requirements. You can choose to work without an application, leveraging automated processes, or opt for a more integrated approach using an application for data handling and validation.

Without an application

If you prefer a streamlined process without the use of an application, it is entirely possible to create bibliographic records using a Power Automate flow alone (Lowagie, 2023a). The concept here is straightforward: the process begins when a file is created. From there, AI models are used to extract the necessary information from the file. Once the data has been extracted, you proceed to work with it, performing various operations that we'll cover in more detail later.

After processing, all the extracted and refined information is consolidated into a single file, often in a format like MARCXML. This consolidated file is then prepared for immediate import into your LMS. If your LMS supports API integration, you can use the API to directly upload the file, ensuring a seamless and automated transfer. Alternatively, if API access is not available, a workaround involves using FTP. In this case, the file is sent to your FTP server, where the LMS can pick it up and import it into the system. This approach ensures that the entire process – from scanning to LMS integration – is efficient and well-organised. By leveraging AI models and flexible transfer methods, it is possible to achieve a high level of automation and accuracy, minimising manual effort and streamlining the workflow. Moreover, in this workflow, no application or data backup is necessary.

This approach is especially valuable in scenarios where minimal intervention is required. By bypassing the use of an application, you completely remove the need to handle data storage and management within Power Platform itself. This streamlines the process and makes it significantly faster and more straightforward. For specific use cases, such as quick creation of bibliographic records, this method can prove to be the most efficient and practical solution. It eliminates the complexities often associated with app-based workflows, such as configuring databases or managing backend operations, making it ideal for situations where simplicity and speed are paramount.

A significant disadvantage of this approach is that you have no direct control over the data being imported into your catalogue. Any errors in the data must be addressed directly within the catalogue itself, which can be a time-consuming process. This lack of oversight during the import process increases the risk of errors being introduced into your catalogue, potentially leading to inconsistencies or inaccuracies that could impact your workflow. To mitigate these challenges, we will explore an alternative option involving the use of an application. In this scenario, the application acts as an intermediary, providing a crucial layer for data validation and correction before the information is sent to the LMS. By incorporating this additional step, you can ensure that the data being imported is accurate, consistent and properly formatted, significantly reducing the likelihood of errors and improving the overall reliability of your system. This approach enhances data quality and streamlines the process by allowing issues to be addressed before they affect your catalogue, saving time and effort in the long run.

With an application

For those who prefer a more comprehensive workflow, it is possible to incorporate an application to manage your data. When using an application to validate your data, you encounter scenarios where users may need to revisit the same record multiple times. For example, a user might need to pause their work to seek advice from a colleague, start processing a record but finish it later or handle cases where the creation of records and their validation occur at different times. These scenarios highlight the need for flexibility in the data validation process, ensuring that users can return to and complete their tasks without losing progress. This necessity introduces a key difference from the 'non-application' method: working with an application inherently requires data storage.

Unlike the direct import approach, where data storage is unnecessary because the information is sent straight to the catalogue, the application-based method relies on a dedicated data storage system. This system allows the data to be saved, retrieved, corrected and exported as needed, providing a controlled environment for validation and refinement. An added layer of data storage ensures that users can work efficiently and accurately, addressing potential errors or adjusting before exporting the data to the catalogue. While this method involves more infrastructure and planning, it also offers significant advantages in terms of flexibility, reliability and the ability to manage and validate records with greater precision.

There are several options for data storage, depending on your requirements and preferences. Popular choices include a Dataverse table, an Excel file or even a Google Sheet, all of which are fully supported by Power Apps and Power Automate. These options provide flexibility, scalability and ease of use, allowing you to select the method that best suits your specific needs and workflow. The data stored in these tables can be easily accessed, viewed and corrected directly from Power Apps. Power Apps provides an intuitive interface where users can display stored data in customisable forms, tables or dashboards. Users can filter, sort and search records to find specific entries quickly. Users can also make real-time updates or corrections to records directly through the app, create new entries in the data table from within the app or delete an entry, ensuring the data remains centralised and up to date. By connecting the app to these data tables, users can manage data efficiently without needing to switch between different tools or platforms.

Each storage method comes with its own advantages, so your choice should align with factors such as data volume, complexity, integration requirements and your organisation's existing infrastructure. Dataverse has versatile column options, which offer a wide range of possibilities for data management. You can create columns to store different types of data, such as files, numbers, text, dates and more, providing flexibility to tailor the database to your specific needs. This adaptability makes Dataverse an ideal choice for scenarios where diverse data types need to be handled efficiently within a single platform, like the extracted text, but also the scans of the document. Dataverse enables you to structure and organise your data in a way that best supports your application's requirements and functionality. Moreover, the fact that Dataverse is integrated within the same Power Platform environment enhances the connection and flow between the data and the application. This integration ensures that data can be easily accessed and transferred between different components of the platform, resulting in smoother workflows and more efficient app performance. By being part of a unified environment, Dataverse simplifies the process of linking data sources to applications, reducing the complexity of managing separate systems. This improves overall functionality. Moreover, it allows for quicker updates, better synchronisation and more reliable data handling across the entire platform.

If you decide to use Excel, it is crucial to note that a simple worksheet alone will not be sufficient. You must create a table within the worksheet and give it a proper name as only named tables can be integrated into your Power Apps application.

This flexible approach allows you to design a workflow that fits your requirements, whether you need a straightforward, file-based process or a more sophisticated, application-driven one. Each option has its advantages depending on the complexity of your data, the necessity for validation and the level of user interaction you desire. By carefully considering these factors, you can create a solution that is both efficient and tailored to your needs, ensuring smooth data handling and integration with your LMS or other systems. Once your database is set up, you can use a Gallery control within Power Apps to display or edit data from your chosen source.

Step-by-step guide: building a cataloguing application

Introduction to the application

After this general introduction, it is time to shift our focus to how these tools can be applied specifically in libraries and cataloguing processes. This guide is made for librarians who may not have a technical background in coding but are eager to take advantage of automation and custom applications to enhance their daily cataloguing tasks. Throughout the guide, you will learn how to use these tools step by step, with practical, hands-on examples designed to meet the unique needs of libraries. By following this guide, you will be equipped to streamline workflows and improve efficiency, all while maintaining high standards of bibliographic records and library management.

We are going to develop an application based on the following scenario: you have a backlog of uncatalogued items (books) and you want to integrate them into your LMS. To accomplish this, we will start by scanning the books using an external scanning application. Once the books are scanned, we will use a Power App to validate the metadata with a laptop, ensuring that the information is accurate and complete. This app will also allow us to add and correct any metadata that may be missing or incorrect. After the metadata is properly validated and edited, we will export the data in the MARCXML format, a standard for bibliographic data exchange. This file will then be sent via FTP protocol because our LMS can directly import MARCXML files. In your LMS, you will be able to see the complete scan, important for later validation of the record. This entire process will help streamline the addition of non-catalogued books into the LMS. We will walk through the process step-by-step to ensure a clear understanding of what needs to be done to create this application. Each stage will be thoroughly explained, from scanning and metadata management to exporting and importing the final data, making it easy to follow along and implement.

When developing an application, the first step is to set up a working environment. This is a crucial part of the process as the environment serves as the platform where you will build and test your application. To create your environment, begin by navigating to the Microsoft Power Platform Admin Center at https://admin.powerplatform.microsoft.com/home. Once there, locate and select the option labelled 'Environment' and then click on '+ New', 'New Environment'. You have the option to start with a developer environment, which is ideal for personal use or small projects. This type of environment is free and provides all the necessary tools for building and testing your app without the need for a paid subscription. It's an excellent starting point, especially if you're new to the platform or just experimenting with app development.

Setting up the environment is an essential step in ensuring that you have all the necessary resources and permissions to begin building your application efficiently. Take time to customise the environment settings as needed for your project as this will ensure a smooth development experience. After setting up your environment, the next step is to navigate to https://make.powerapps.com. This is where you will begin creating and managing your application. Once on the site, select the environment you have just created from the drop-down menu located on the top navigation bar. Choosing the correct environment is crucial as this determines the context in which your app will be developed and managed. To proceed, log in using an account that has the appropriate licenses and permissions. This step is essential because your access to key features and tools needed for app development depends on the type of licenses associated with your account. Certain advanced capabilities may only be available if you have a Power Apps plan or an equivalent license. Double-check that your chosen environment is the one intended for your project as working in the wrong environment could lead to confusion or mismanagement of resources later on. With the proper setup and access, you are now ready to explore the interface and begin the exciting process of building your app.

1. Start the process by creating a Solution, which serves as a container that allows you to organise and manage all related components in one place, such as tables, AI models and apps.
2. Set up a Dataverse table that will serve as the foundation for your data storage and management. This table will hold the records you want to analyse, store metadata and link to other components of your system.
3. Next, create your AI models, train them, and publish them so they can be used in your flow.
4. With all components now ready, you can design and implement your Power Automate flows to streamline and automate your processes.

   - Power Automate Flow 'Analyse': This flow will be responsible for analysing the images, extracting relevant metadata and performing HTTP queries to enrich the data. It will also handle subject indexing to categorise the records appropriately before saving the data back to the Dataverse table.
   - Two Power Automate flows that can be used for subject indexing and entity extraction, providing an additional layer of intelligence and organisation to your data. While these flows are not strictly mandatory, they can significantly enhance the overall quality and usefulness of the final output.

- Power Automate Flow 'CreateRecord': This flow will focus on creating a file based on the processed data and then sending this file to your LMS. This ensures that the data is accessible and can be used for educational purposes or further analysis.

5 Finally, create a Power App that allows users to interact with the data in a user-friendly way. This app can be designed to provide easy access to the data stored in your Dataverse table and create your output file.

By following these steps, you can set up a robust system that automates the handling and analysis of data, integrates with your LMS and provides an intuitive interface for end-users through the Power App.

Create your solution

Using a solution offers several benefits, particularly when exporting it to different environments. It enables seamless portability and ensures that all the components function together as intended. One of the key advantages of using a solution is the ability to include variables, such as the URL of your SharePoint site. This feature simplifies the management of dynamic elements within your flow. For example, you can define a variable for the SharePoint URL and use it throughout your flow. If the URL changes in the future, you only need to update the variable in one place. This update will automatically propagate to all instances where the variable is referenced, ensuring that your flow remains accurate and up to date without requiring manual adjustments in multiple locations. Overall, creating a solution helps organise your project components efficiently. It makes maintenance and updates significantly easier, providing a flexible and scalable framework for managing your resources.

To add a new solution, follow these simple steps. Begin by navigating to the left-hand menu and clicking on '... More'. From there, select 'Solutions' and then click 'New Solution' at the top of the page. You'll be prompted to provide a name for your solution, choose a publisher and, once those are selected, your solution will be created. The first step once inside your newly created solution is to add a solution variable. This is especially useful if you will be frequently connecting to specific external resources, such as a SharePoint site. For example, if you plan to connect to a SharePoint site, you can store that site's URL as a variable within the solution for easy reference later. To do this, click on 'New', then 'More', followed by 'Environment Variable'. When configuring the environment variable for a SharePoint connection, select 'Data Source' as the data type, choose 'Site' as the type and input the SharePoint URL into the 'Current Site' field. This creates a reusable variable that can be easily referenced in your flows and apps. It is important to note that any apps, Dataverse tables and flows you plan to use with your solution should also be created from within this solution. Doing so allows you to use the environment variables you have defined within your flows and apps, making your processes more dynamic and adaptable. Another important component are connection references. These complement environment variables by providing a reusable authentication mechanism for connectors like SharePoint, Outlook or Dataverse. It ensures that flows and apps can securely access data sources without requiring individual authentication setups for each use case. When exporting and importing solutions, connection references help preserve connections without breaking workflows, making it easier to move automations between development, testing and production environments. To create any of these components, simply click on 'New' at the top of the solution page and select what you want to add, whether it is a new app, a Dataverse table or a flow. By centralising everything within the solution, you ensure seamless integration across your environment and make it easier to manage and update all components in the future.

Create your Dataverse table

To get started with creating your table, open your solution and click on the 'New' button, followed by selecting 'Table'. When prompted with different options, choose 'Start from blank'. This will give you the flexibility to design your table exactly as you need, beginning with a completely empty structure. Next, you will need to name your table. Choose a name that clearly reflects the type of information it will contain as this will help keep your project organised and make it easier for others to understand the table's purpose at a glance. For example, if you are creating a table to store information about books, a straightforward and descriptive name like 'Book' would work well. Remember, the name you select can be crucial for organisation, especially if your project includes multiple tables or complex data. A well-chosen name makes it simpler to locate and work with the data later. For even better organisation, consider including an acronym or abbreviation of your institution in the table's name. This is especially helpful if you are working within a shared environment or managing multiple projects as it helps distinguish your tables from those created by others. For example, since at KBR, we would name the table 'kbr Book'. Adding the institution's acronym keeps things tidy but also makes it instantly clear where the table originates. This small adjustment can be particularly valuable in collaborative settings, where multiple teams or departments may be accessing and managing similar types of data. Modify the name using the 'Properties' button, preferably before saving. This ensures that the column for the unique identifier reflects your chosen name, which will be important later.

When designing a table, it is essential to use clear and concise headers to ensure that the contents of each cell are easily understood. It is recommended that you use short, descriptive titles that communicate the necessary information without being too wordy. For example, instead of using a long header like 'place of publication' simply use 'place'. It is also recommended that you use headers such as 'title', 'subtitle', 'place', 'year', 'publisher', 'edition' and 'publisher' for a table containing bibliographic information. These brief and precise labels help maintain a clean and organised table layout. That is more practical to work with, especially when you have to use them in different places (application, flow). If you are working with MARC21, consider using MARC21 fields as your table headers. This approach can simplify your workflow, especially if you plan to export the data to a MARC21XML format later. By setting up your headers in MARC21 format from the beginning, you create a structure that aligns with standard bibliographic records, making future data transfers and conversions smoother and less time-consuming. For example, headers in this format might look like '245$a' for the title, '245$b' for the remainder of the title, '245$c' for the statement of responsibility, '264$a' for the place of publication, '264$b' for the publisher, '264$c' for the publication date and so forth. Structuring your table in this way ensures compatibility with MARC21 standards, making it easier to maintain and export records with minimal adjustments. This method also enhances the clarity and accuracy of your data organisation, allowing others familiar with MARC21 to navigate and understand the table structure more intuitively.

For each column in your table, it is essential to define the data type, as outlined in Chapter 2. Choosing the correct data type for each column ensures that your table accurately handles the specific type of information stored there, whether it is plain text, numbers, dates or more complex data. Defining data types at this stage improves data integrity and enhances the table's functionality, making it easier to perform searches, sort data or apply filters later. Properly defined data types will help prevent errors and ensure that the table remains compatible with any automated processes or exports you might need in the future. Since our columns will primarily store descriptive information, such as book titles or author names, use the Dataverse data type 'Text: Single line of Text' for these fields. This data type is ideal for handling text entries like titles, author names and other descriptive details. It ensures that the information is stored in a consistent, readable format, without any issues related to formatting or conversion. For the year of publication, you might consider using the Number data type, especially if you need to store only the numerical year (e.g., 2025). However, be cautious when using this data type as it can cause errors in certain cases. For example, if the data is not entered in the expected format or is not properly converted, it can lead to issues. Additionally, if the year is entered in Roman numerals (like MMXXV) or if the field includes additional information such as 'April 2025' rather than just the year, these variations can cause conversion problems. In such cases, it is often safer to use the Text data type, even for years, to avoid potential errors and ensure that all possible formats and variations are accommodated properly.

I suggest increasing the default maximum character limit, which is by default set to 100, to 3,000. A limit of 100 characters is often too restrictive, especially for fields that require more detailed information, such as the CoverURL or Title fields. For example, a book's title might be longer than 100 characters. Similarly, URLs for cover images or other online resources can easily exceed this limit. By extending the character limit to 3,000, you ensure that there is enough space for more comprehensive entries, avoiding the need to truncate information or store it across multiple fields. Expanding the character limit to 3,000 would provide greater flexibility, avoiding errors and ensuring that all necessary details can be included without restrictions. This change future-proofs the table for handling larger datasets or more descriptive content, contributing to the overall reliability and usability of your database.

The Table 4.1 opposite provides an overview of a possible Dataverse table structure. For this demo, we are using descriptive column headers, instead of the MARC21 tags, for clarity and ease of understanding. How the content of the table will be generated is also outlined. The data can be sourced from a variety of methods, including technical metadata form the detected file (URL for the cover), from the output from the used AI models or manually Encoded Information. This shows that the table can be populated through a combination of automated and manual methods, depending on the specific needs and available data sources. By leveraging automated processes such as AI model extraction or HTTP queries, alongside manually encoded information when necessary, we can ensure that the bibliographic record is as complete and accurate as possible. This method results in a rich, well-rounded bibliographic entry that reflects all available and relevant information, making the record more valuable for cataloguing, searching and future use.

Table 4.1 *Possible columns in our Dataverse table*

Dataverse Column Header	**Data Population Method**	**Description**
CoverURL	Generated from Scan	This will be used to put in the URL of the thumbnail.
*Title**	AI TitlePage	AI-detected title page.
*Subtitle**	AI TitlePage	
*Author1**	AI TitlePage	
*Author2**	AI TitlePage	Sometimes, a title page may list the author and title together, followed by a separate statement of responsibility, such as 'translated by'. In such cases, it is a good idea to split this information into two distinct columns: one for the author and title and another for the additional details, e.g., the translator's name. This separation makes the data easier to organise and work with initially. Later on, if needed, you can always combine these two columns into a single field using a semicolon to separate the different elements. For example, you might merge them as 'Author ; translated by [Translator's Name]'. This approach allows for greater flexibility in managing and formatting your data, ensuring clarity and consistency throughout your work.
*Edition**	AI TitlePage	
*Place**	AI TitlePage or AI CopyrightPage	In older books, the place of publication is typically found on the title page. However, in modern publications, this information is often relegated to the copyright page.
*Publisher**	AI TitlePage	
*Year**	AI TitlePage or AI CopyrightPage	In older books, the year of publication is typically found on the title page. However, in modern publications, this information is often relegated to the copyright page.
*ISBN**	AI CopyrightPage	
*ISSN**	AI CopyrightPage	
*LegalDepositNumber**	AI CopyrightPage	
*SubjectText**	Text recognition	Text from back cover (or if using external sources, the value from the summary of that record (e.g., field 520$a)).
Extracted_Entities_ Summary_City	AI Entity Extraction	
Extracted_Entities_ Summary_Person	AI Entity Extraction	
*Subject_Terms**	AI Category Classification	
*NumberOfPages**	Manually App	Optional: can be added via the application.
*Measurements**	Manually App	Optional: can be added via the application.
*Bibliography, Etc (optional)**	Manually App	Information indicating the presence of one or more bibliographies, discographies, filmographies or other bibliographic references within the described item or in any accompanying materials. Optional: can be added via the application.
*MARC21-fields from external sources**	HTTP searches	

All fields marked with an asterisk (*) can be populated through HTTP queries if an ISBN is detected and a record is found in an external database. This allows for efficient integration of comprehensive data directly into the final output, as detailed in the section on HTTP searches.

Create your AI models

To effectively process and catalogue your documents, it is essential to create and train AI models tailored to specific types of information. Each model should be specialised to extract particular data points accurately, streamlining the workflow and ensuring consistency across your records. Below is a detailed guide on how to set up your different AI models. To achieve our objectives, we will need to develop at least two AI models, with each tailored to a specific task. The first model will focus on extracting information from the title page, while the second will specialise in extracting details from the copyright page. Additionally, there is the option to create a third model or connection with a prompt for subject indexing, but we will delve into this possibility later under the section 'Optional: Subject Indexing and Entity Extraction'.

The process begins with creating and training an AI model dedicated to extracting information from the title page. To do this, navigate to AI Hub and select the Document Processing Model. Follow the detailed instructions provided in Chapter 3 to ensure a smooth setup, including defining the fields to extract, organising your training set into collections, annotating the documents and training the model. Once the model is trained, rename it to 'TitlePage'. This model should be designed to identify and extract critical elements from the title page, such as the title, subtitle, author and publisher.

After setting up the 'TitlePage' model, proceed to create the second AI model focused on extracting information from the copyright page. Rename this model to 'CopyrightPage'. Setting up the model for copyright pages follows a similar process to that of the title page model, but it comes with unique challenges. While the title page allows for the creation of multiple collections to represent the diversity in layouts and formats, copyright pages present a more complex scenario. Their structure and content can vary significantly across publications, making it difficult to categorise and group them into distinct collections. Due to these complexities, you can streamline the process by creating a single collection for copyright pages. This approach ensures that the model is exposed to a broad range of examples without the added difficulty of managing multiple collections. Of course, after training KBR's model using this approach, we tested its performance. The results were promising; the copyright page model demonstrated its ability to accurately extract the most important information from the data. Key details, such as publication year, ISBN, ISSN and legal deposit number, were successfully identified and processed. Given this level of success, there was no immediate need to refine either the model itself or the collection setup. The single collection approach appears to have provided sufficient variety and coverage for the model to perform effectively, ensuring reliable and consistent results in extracting critical publication details from copyright pages.

By creating and training these specialised AI models using 'TitlePage' for the title information and 'CopyrightPage' for detailed publication data, we can automate the extraction of critical bibliographic data from title and copyright pages with high precision. This can significantly streamline your cataloguing process. These models work together to automate data extraction, reduce manual input and ensure that each document is comprehensively and accurately represented in your system. Investing time in the initial setup and training of these AI models will pay off in the long run by increasing efficiency, reducing errors and enhancing the quality of your bibliographic records. As you refine and update these models over time (retraining them with extra examples), they will continue to improve, further supporting your goal of creating a robust cataloguing system.

AI models are one of the few components that can't be directly created from within a solution. Therefore, once you have built your AI models outside of the solution, you can easily integrate them. To do this, go to your solution, click on 'Add Existing' and select your AI models from the list. This step will add the models to your solution, ensuring they are available for use in your flows, apps or other processes within the solution.

Create your Power Automate flows

After you have created your Dataverse table, the next step is to set up your flows. To do this, go to your solution and click on 'New' – 'Automation'. You will be presented with different types of flows to choose from. We only want to use a cloud flow. Cloud flows are designed to automate tasks and processes across various online services, such as Microsoft 365, Dynamics 365 or any other cloud-based application. They can be triggered by specific events, such as receiving an e-mail or when a new item is added to your Dataverse table, and can perform actions like sending notifications, updating records or integrating data between different systems. Cloud flows are particularly useful for automating workflows that involve cloud services and need to operate in real-time.

When creating a flow, you will have three options to choose from: an automated cloud flow; an instant cloud flow; or a scheduled cloud flow. An automated cloud flow operates based on specific triggers, such as an event occurring in another application (for example, 'a file is created in SharePoint'), making it ideal for processes that need to run automatically. An instant cloud flow, on the other hand, allows you to trigger actions immediately with a simple button click or a manual event, providing quick responses to user input. Lastly, a scheduled cloud flow is set to run at designated intervals, allowing you to automate tasks like sending reports or updates at regular times. If you are unsure of how to set up one of those cloud flows, you can describe your requirements in plain language and the Copilot feature will analyse your description and create a flow based on your input. This can be particularly helpful for users who may not be familiar with the technical details of flow creation.

Preliminary step: organising your SharePoint site

A key step in preparing for a smooth workflow that connects with a SharePoint site, is to organise your SharePoint site effectively. SharePoint is an excellent tool for collaborative work because it allows team members to share, access and manage documents in real time, enhancing productivity and reducing the need for back-and-forth e-mails or managing local, duplicate copies. By centralising files in one accessible location, SharePoint makes it easy for everyone involved in a project to stay aligned, ensuring that each team member always has the latest version of every document.

To set up your SharePoint for this purpose, create a new Document Library named 'Cataloguing'. This library will serve as the main repository for all documents related to the cataloguing process. Within this Document Library, it is helpful to create three specific folders that represent the key stages of your workflow. These folders will make it easier to track documents as they move through each stage of the process, providing a clear structure and helping the team to quickly see the status of each file at any given time. Setting up these folders in advance improves organisation and simplifies tracking and troubleshooting down the line. This way, if an issue arises, team members can locate the file easily and see exactly where it may have stalled in the process. Overall, this structure will help streamline collaboration and keep the project progressing smoothly, even when multiple people are working on it. Possible folders in the Document Library can be:

1 'Scans': This folder is designated for holding all new scans that are ready to be processed. It serves as the initial drop-off point for incoming files, which can be automatically sent here via a document scanning application, such as OneDrive or Microsoft Lens. By centralising new scans in this folder, the team can easily keep track of which files have

been added and are awaiting processing, ensuring that no new documents are overlooked. The Power Automate flow is set to trigger automatically whenever a new file is added to this folder. This automated activation streamlines the workflow, ensuring that each new file immediately initiates the necessary processing steps without any manual intervention. By triggering as soon as a file enters the folder, the flow helps maintain an efficient, real-time processing pipeline that minimises delays and keeps tasks moving forward smoothly. This setup is particularly beneficial for high-volume environments as it ensures each new document is promptly processed and ready for the next stage.

2 'Processing': This folder is reserved for PDFs that are currently undergoing the processing stage. As files move from 'Scans' to 'Processing', they are actively being worked on, whether for data extraction, formatting or another processing task. This folder also plays a key role in troubleshooting; if a file remains in the 'Processing' folder for an extended period, it may signal an issue in the workflow that's preventing the file from advancing to the next stage. By regularly monitoring this folder, the team can identify potential bottlenecks and resolve issues before they impact the entire process.

3 'Processed': This folder is for files that have successfully completed the scanning and processing stages. Once a file is placed in the 'Processed' folder, it signals that the bibliographic record is created and the scan is ready for further use or archiving. To improve organisation and accessibility, it can be helpful to rename each file added to this folder. Consider incorporating specific identifiers in the file name, for example, extracted metadata from the scan itself (such as the ISBN or other relevant bibliographic data). This makes it easier to locate and reference files in the future, especially when handling large volumes of documents.

These three folders represent the sequential stages in the process, providing an easy way to track the status of each file as it moves from one stage to the next. By structuring your folders this way – 'Scans', 'Processing' and 'Processed' – you create a streamlined workflow that aids in monitoring and troubleshooting the process at each stage. This way, any delays or issues are easier to identify, enabling you to resolve them efficiently and keep the process moving smoothly.

Preliminary step: organising the scanning process

Before diving into the step-by-step explanation of how to create the flow, it is helpful to have a brief overview of the scanning process. Understanding this process will give you a clearer foundation and help you follow along with the flow creation more effectively. This context will make it easier to implement each step confidently, ensuring you understand what to do and why each action is necessary.

It is crucial to handle a scan as a single unit because separating images can complicate the post-processing steps. Moreover, scanning images separately may involve multiple steps in the scanning workflow, such as sending each scan individually, which is not efficient. To simplify this process, you can scan an entire document into a single PDF file using an application like OneDrive's built-in document scanner. This application allows you to scan multiple pages and combine them into one cohesive PDF document. Once the PDF is created, it can be conveniently uploaded to either OneDrive or SharePoint. This approach ensures that all related images are grouped together, making it easier to manage and retrieve them later. By scanning documents as one PDF, we reduce the complexity of handling the files, streamline the scanning process and maintain the integrity of the data during storage and retrieval.

It is essential to ensure that the scans are captured in a consistent order throughout this process because the flow requires assigning an AI model to specific pages. We will go into more detail on this later, but for now, it is critical that all your scans follow the same structure to ensure accuracy. Here is the recommended sequence for your scans:

1 Page 1 – Cover: The first page of the scan should be the cover of the document. This serves as the visual representation in the application, making it easier for users to identify the document at a glance. A clear image of the cover helps with visual recognition and provides a reference for verifying the physical appearance of the document, such as its design, colour scheme and any unique elements like illustrations or logos.
2 Page 2 – Title Page: The title page will be processed by the first AI model to accurately identify and capture essential details, such as the title, author, subtitle and publisher. The AI model 'TitlePage' is trained to recognise and extract this data, which forms the foundation of the bibliographic record. This structured information is vital for cataloguing purposes and enhances searchability within the system. By automating this process, we can ensure consistency and reduce the manual effort required to input these details.
3 Page 3 – Copyright page: The copyright page, usually located at the end of the book or on the reverse of the title page, will be treated with the AI model 'CopyrightPage'. The copyright page contains important metadata about the document, information such as the ISBN, publication year, place

of publication, publisher's address and website, legal deposit number and other details that are crucial for cataloguing. Some information may occasionally be found on the title page, while in other cases it is located on the copyright page. The distribution of information often varies depending on the publication date of the book. Older books typically include more detailed information on the title page, such as the full title, author's name and sometimes even the publisher and year of publication. In contrast, contemporary books tend to have more streamlined title pages that focus on the essentials, such as the title and author, with additional details being provided in an expanded copyright page. This shift reflects a change in the standard layout of books, where the title page is now more focused on presenting the title and author prominently, while the copyright page serves as a dedicated space for more technical publishing details. This evolution in the placement of publication information underscores the importance of checking different parts of a book when cataloguing to ensure that all relevant details are accurately captured.

4 Page 4 – Back Cover: The back cover often contains descriptive text that can be valuable for subject indexing. This page will be processed by an 'Extract text' model. This text may include summaries, keywords or other content that provides insight into the document's themes and topics. This text can then be used for subject indexing.
5 Page 5 and beyond – Additional Pages. Beyond the essential pages, you may include any additional pages that you consider important. These could be appendices, tables of contents, introduction pages or any other content that adds value to the record. Including these pages can provide a more comprehensive view of the document and ensure that any supplementary information is also captured. This is particularly useful for documents that have significant content beyond the main narrative, such as charts, graphs or supplementary texts. By scanning these pages, we ensure that all relevant information is available for cataloguing and future reference, making the record as complete and useful as possible.

This structured scanning approach ensures that all critical aspects of the document are captured in a systematic and comprehensive manner. From visual identification with the cover page to detailed metadata extraction from the copyright page and subject indexing from the back cover, each page serves a specific purpose. This method facilitates efficient and accurate cataloguing. Maintaining this order will allow the AI model to accurately interpret each page's content based on its predetermined position in the sequence. To minimise the number of scans, you can opt to create a basic bibliographic record using just the title and copyright pages. However, since the scan will be displayed in the LMS so that it can also be used by a human cataloguer to verify and validate the record, it can be beneficial to include a few additional scans beyond the basic ones. This will provide more comprehensive documentation, making it easier for the cataloguer to cross-check the details and confirm the accuracy of the catalogued data. This approach aids the cataloguer in validating more effectively and creating a more thorough and reliable record based on the scan.

Once you have defined your scanning process and the sequence in which scans should be handled and organised your SharePoint site accordingly, you can proceed to create your flows in Power Automate.

Power Automate flow 'Analyse' (before validation in the application)

This flow is one of the most crucial steps, as it is designed to extract and store the bibliographic metadata for further processing and automation. When the flow is triggered, it will retrieve the documents stored in the 'Scan' folder and capture their content. The document will then be analysed, using AI models to identify the key bibliographic fields. The metadata generated from this analysis will be used to perform HTTP searches, enabling the retrieval of additional data or verification of existing information. Finally, all processed data will be systematically stored in a Dataverse table, creating a centralised and organised repository where all metadata details are stored. By doing so, the metadata becomes accessible and can be easily viewed, updated or modified within the Power App. This integration with Power Apps enhances the flexibility of the system as team members can interact with and refine the metadata as needed. This streamlined flow ensures that each scanned file is processed efficiently, with all relevant information readily available for ongoing use.

Trigger and get files

The trigger for our workflow is a click on a button in the Power App, so you will need to add the 'Power Apps (V2)' trigger. While it is possible to add an input to be sent from Power App to the flow, it is not necessary for this particular flow since no information needs to be sent from Power Apps to the flow (though you will need inputs for the second workflow, which will be discussed later). The next step involves listing files from a specific folder in a SharePoint document library. To do this, add the action 'Get files (properties only)'. This action scans a designated folder and retrieves a list of all the files stored within it. You will need to provide specific parameters to tell the flow where to look for the files. First, you need to fill in the Site Address. This is the address of the SharePoint site where the files are stored. You can either select the site directly or choose 'Enter custom value' to use an environment variable that contains the SharePoint Site URL. As mentioned, using an environment variable ensures that the URL is dynamic and can change depending on the environment. Next, specify the document library and the folder within that library where the files are located.

Move file to 'Processing' folder

After doing this, you need to process all the files in that folder. For each file, start by moving the PDF file to the 'Processing' folder. This step indicates that the document is currently being processed and that the workflow has begun. This is an important step to visually organise files and ensure smooth workflow execution, while avoiding duplicate processing. There are five fields that need to be completed for this action:

1. Current SharePoint Address: Select the appropriate SharePoint site address either from the list or by using the environment variable.
2. File to Move: You will need to specify which file should be moved. To do this, select the 'Identifier' from the Dynamic Content section of the 'Get files (properties only)' action. (Be sure to select 'Identifier', not 'ID', as they are two different properties.) When this is done, a loop will automatically be created by adding an 'Apply to each' section. This makes sense as the flow will not move just one file but all the files from the specified folder. All subsequent actions will be nested inside this 'Apply to each' component, allowing the flow to process each file in the folder efficiently. This ensures that every file goes through the same steps in the workflow.
3. Destination Site Address: This is usually the same SharePoint site as the source, but if necessary, it can be a different site where the file will be moved to.
4. Destination Folder: In this field, specify the folder where the file should be moved. In this case, it will be the 'Processing' folder.
5. The last field determines what happens if a file with the same name already exists in the destination folder. Since the external application KBR work with generates unique file names, we chose the 'fail this action' option, which will cause the flow to stop if a duplicate is detected. This helps signal that something went wrong, allowing us to investigate the issue. However, depending on your needs, you could also choose other options, such as creating a copy with a different name or moving the file to another location.

Get file content

The next step is to retrieve the content of the newly created file. To do this, add the action 'Get file content – SharePoint'. In the Site Address field, select your SharePoint site address (direct or using the environment variable). For the File Identifier, go to the Dynamic Content panel and choose the 'Id' from the 'Move File' action. This will retrieve the file content for further processing.

Extract information from title and copyright pages

Now that you have the file content, it needs to be analysed by the AI models. You can do this by adding the 'Extract information from Documents' action. In this step, select the AI model that will process the document. Choose the AI model named TitlePage as this model is designed to extract the relevant data. For the Form Type, select 'PDF Document'. In the Form field, choose 'File Content' from the 'Get file content – SharePoint' action. Open 'Show advanced options' and on pages put '2' (this reflects how we ordered the PDF with the title page on the second page of the PDF). Rename the action to 'Extract information from title page'. By setting up these actions, you ensure that the content of the uploaded file is retrieved and processed efficiently using AI. This structure allows the AI model to extract specific information from the PDF document, streamlining your workflow and automating the analysis of the file.

Next, you will need to analyse the copyright page, but this can be done simultaneously with the analysis of the title page. To do this, click on the small arrow located above the current action. A 'plus' icon (+) will appear, along with two options: 'Add an action' and 'Add a parallel branch'. The 'Add an action' option allows you to insert an additional step between two previously defined actions. The 'Add a parallel branch' allows you to run multiple actions simultaneously, instead of in a sequential, step-by-step manner. This can significantly improve the efficiency of your workflow, especially when you want certain tasks or processes to be executed at the same time. Normally, actions are carried out one after another in chronological order. This means if you have multiple actions, each one has to complete before the next one can start. However, when you're working with multiple AI models or processes that can function independently, this sequential approach can be time-consuming. If you do this sequentially, first the AI model will analyse the title page, then it will move on to the copyright page. This would take more time since the second step has to wait for the first one to finish. However, with a parallel branch, both extractions happen at the same time, so you complete both tasks in the time it takes to finish the slower of the two processes, saving a lot of time compared to sequential execution. By running tasks concurrently, you make better use of Power Automate's processing power. So, if two or more tasks do not depend on each other's output, run them in parallel.

So, in this case, select 'Add a parallel branch'. Once you have done that, choose the action 'Extract information from documents' again. You can rename this action to 'Extract information from copyright page' to make it more specific. After that, select the AI model 'CopyrightPage' and for the form type, choose 'PDF Document' again. Next, for the 'Form' field, you will need to reference the content retrieved from the previous 'Get file content – SharePoint' action. To ensure the correct page is treated, open the advanced options and enter '3' in the field 'Page', indicating that the extraction should occur on page 3. By following these steps, you'll be able to efficiently set up the simultaneous extraction of information from both the title and copyright pages.

Recognise the text from back cover

A third parallel branch could be created to extract the text from the back cover, which is on page 4 of the scanned document. To do this, add a third parallel branch and select the action 'Recognize text in an image or a PDF document'. Rename this action to 'Get text from back cover' to keep the process clear and organised. Next, select the File Content from the 'Get file content – SharePoint' action, ensuring that you are working with the correct document. One challenge with this step is that the action will, by default, extract text from the entire PDF, not just page 4.

To implement this process, start by returning to the beginning of the workflow and creating a new string variable named 'BackCoverText'. Now we want to append the content extracted from page 4 to the newly created variable. To achieve this, you will need to introduce a condition that verifies whether the extracted text is specifically from page 4. In this condition, use the 'Item' field from the output of the 'Get text from back cover' action. When you do this, the system will automatically generate an 'Apply to each' action with the output named 'Results', allowing it to loop through the extracted data. Within this loop, the condition will check the 'Item-page' value to confirm if it corresponds to page 4. Rename the created 'Apply to each' action to 'CheckPages'. Then, adjust the condition so that it specifically evaluates whether the extracted content matches the criteria for page 4 using this expression in the left box of the condition:

```
equals(items('CheckPages')?['page'],4)
```

Keep the default condition set to 'is equal to' and, in the corresponding right-hand box, enter the expression 'true'. This configuration ensures that the system verifies whether the extracted text is from page 4 – commonly the back cover of a document.

Next, within the 'If Yes' condition, create an 'Apply to each' action. Use the output labelled 'lines' from the 'Get text from back cover' action as the input for this loop. The purpose here is to process every line of text individually. For each line, include a 'Compose' action and use the 'Text' output from the current line. Append this text with a blank space to ensure proper formatting and separation between words. Following this, update the variable 'BackCoverText' by adding the output from the 'Compose' action. By doing so, the variable will consolidate all the text from page 4, including each line and word, into a cohesive block of text. This sequence effectively collects all the back cover content in a structured and usable format, starting from the extracted data (referred to as 'Results') and narrowing it down to the specific page ('Items/page') and its individual lines ('Lines'). While the process may initially seem intricate, it becomes straightforward once properly set up. After configuration, the system operates seamlessly, ensuring accurate and efficient extraction of the desired text.

The main tasks in the analysis process are now complete. The next steps involve conducting HTTP searches and transferring the processed data into a Dataverse table for further use or storage. Additionally, there is an optional layer of refinement you can apply to enrich your results – subject indexing and entity extraction – which will be addressed later in the process. Let's now take a closer look at each of these final tasks to ensure a smooth and thorough completion of the analysis process.

Perform HTTP searches

To enhance your dataset by performing an HTTP search, you need a unique identifier that ensures accurate search results. The most reliable value to use for this purpose is an ISBN. While it is technically possible to search by title and author, doing so carries a higher risk of inaccurate or ambiguous results. For the sake of clarity and reliability, we will assume that an ISBN is available. To check for the presence of an ISBN in your data, we need to use the output of the AI model 'CopyrightPage'. If this model has detected an ISBN, we can proceed with the search.

Click on 'New Step' in your workflow and type in 'Condition – Control' to create a new condition. This condition will determine whether an ISBN is present before proceeding further. In the field 'Choose a value', navigate to the tab 'Expression' and type 'empty()'. This expression will allow us to check if the ISBN value is missing or present. After typing 'empty()', click between the parentheses. Then, go to 'Dynamic Content' and select 'ISBN value' from the action that extracted the information from the 'CopyrightPage' model. 'ISBN' is the text field that you defined in the beginning of training your AI model. These labels come back here in the output of the AI model. This should result in a formula like this:

empty(outputs('Extract_information_from_copyrightpage')?['body/responsev2/predictionOutput/labels/ISBN/value'])

Next, select the option 'is equal to' and, in the third field, return to the 'Expression' tab and type in 'false'. This will set up a condition that checks whether the ISBN field is not empty. Once the condition is in place, you will see two branches: 'If Yes' and 'If No'. The 'If Yes' branch indicates that an ISBN is present, while the 'If No' branch means that the ISBN is missing. If an ISBN is available (the 'If Yes' scenario), the workflow can proceed with the HTTP search using that ISBN, ensuring a reliable and accurate search result. On the other hand, if no ISBN is detected (the 'If No' branch), you have the option to configure an HTTP query based on alternative fields such as the title and/or author. However, as mentioned earlier, searching based on title and author can introduce more risks of incorrect matches or ambiguous results. For the purposes of this demonstration, we will not be setting up a search based on title or author. But it is important to note that there may be instances where title or author searches are necessary. Depending on your project's needs, you can customise the 'If No' branch to include this fallback search option or even incorporate error handling to alert you when no ISBN is found, prompting manual intervention.

Click on the 'If Yes' branch, then add a new action. In the search bar, type and select the premium operation 'HTTP'. Since we are using this operation to retrieve information, set the method to 'GET'. The URL you use will depend on the data source or service you wish to query. There are several SRU (Search/Retrieve via URL) services that you can leverage to perform these searches. For example, if you're searching for books with the ISBN '978-1-78330-629-9' (the book *From Cataloguing to Metadata Creation* by Mauro Guerrini), you have a few search options depending on the output format you need. The 'recordSchema' parameter in the URL defines the format of the search results. Here are some examples of SRU queries for various libraries:

- BnF (Bibliothèque nationale de France). You can search the French National Library catalogue using the following URLs:
  - UNIMARC XML format:
    https://catalogue.bnf.fr/api/SRU?version=1.2&operation=searchRetrieve&query=bib.isbn all "9781783306299"&recordSchema=unimarcxchange
  - Dublin Core XML format:
    https://catalogue.bnf.fr/api/SRU?version=1.2&operation=searchRetrieve&query=bib.isbn all "9781783306299"&recordSchema=dublincore

- German National Library (Deutsche Nationalbibliothek, DNB). You can also query the German National Library's catalogue with the following options:
  - RDF XML format: https://services.dnb.de/sru/dnb?version=1.1&operation=searchRetrieve&query=9781783306299&recordSchema=RDFxml
  - MARC21 XML format: https://services.dnb.de/sru/dnb?version=1.1&operation=searchRetrieve&query=9781783306299&recordSchema=MARC21-xml
- Belgian Union Catalogue UniCat:
  - MARC21 XML format: https://unicat.be/sru?version=1.1&operation=searchRetrieve&query=9781783306299&recordSchema=marcxml

The parameters of the URL, such as 'operation', 'query' and 'recordSchema', remain consistent, which is one of the major benefits of using a standardised search and retrieval method like SRU. The only thing that changes is the base server address. This consistency simplifies the process, making it easier to develop and maintain applications that rely on fetching data from different sources. Instead of having to adjust to varying query formats or parameters when interacting with different databases, SRU ensures a uniform approach. This standardisation boosts efficiency and reduces potential errors, making it a highly effective tool for retrieving information across multiple platforms.

By selecting the appropriate SRU service and output format, the data returned is structured in a way that is both relevant and easy to interpret. This approach also provides flexibility in how you choose to integrate the information, depending on the catalogue you are searching and the output schema that best suits your needs.

To set up an external data source for querying, start by identifying the specific URL you will use. This URL will direct your application to the service that provides the data. In this example, we will use the SRU service provided by the German National Library (DNB), which returns records in MARCXML format. To begin, select the action 'HTTP' and select 'GET' – Method. Enter the following URL into the designated URL field:

https://services.dnb.de/sru/dnb?version=1.1&operation=searchRetrieve&query=[ISBN]&recordSchema=MARC21-xml

In this URL:

- 'version=1.1' specifies the SRU protocol version to be used
- 'operation=searchRetrieve' defines the request as a search query
- 'query=[ISBN]' is where you'll insert the specific ISBN value or other search parameter. Here, you select 'Dynamic content' and select from the output from the AI model 'CopyrightPage' the ISBN value.
- 'recordSchema=MARC21-xml' tells the service to return the data in MARCXML format.

If you want to perform a search without the hyphens or spaces that can be found in an ISBN, instead of dynamic content you can choose the 'expression' tab and add an expression that deletes the hyphens and spaces:

> *replace(replace([Put here the ISBN value from your copyright page model output using dynamic input],' ', ''),'-','')*

For this service, add the following line to the headers section: Left: Accept, Right: /. This header ensures that the server accepts any type of response format, allowing for maximum flexibility in handling the incoming data. By setting up these details carefully, your application will be able to communicate effectively with the DNB's SRU service and retrieve accurate bibliographic data.

To store the result of your query efficiently, it is best to place it into a string variable. In this process, variables need to be defined at the start of the workflow. So, first, go back to the beginning of your flow. After the trigger action, add an 'Initialize Variable' action to set up a string variable that will hold the query result. In the 'Initialize Variable' action, set the type to 'String'. This variable will initially be empty and will eventually store the result of the HTTP query from the DNB. Choose a clear and descriptive name for this variable, such as 'ResultDNB', so that the content and purpose of the variable are easy to identify. Next, navigate back to the HTTP query you have set up for the DNB. After configuring this query, add the action 'Append to String Variable'. This step allows you to transfer the result from the HTTP query into the string variable you created. In the 'Append to String Variable' action, select the string variable you just initialised, 'ResultDNB'. Then, for the value, use the 'Body' output from the HTTP action. This approach ensures that the full response from the DNB search is stored in your variable. It is worth noting that while you may have only one variable at this stage, you might add additional variables, for example, if you plan to query multiple sources. Naming each variable descriptively will help you keep track of what each one contains, which is crucial when managing complex workflows. This setup makes it easy to access and use your query results throughout the rest of the flow.

Once you have stored the query result in the variable, you can begin extracting specific information from it. Since the output format we chose is MARCXML, we will use an XPath expression to locate and retrieve the desired information from the XML structure. XPath is a powerful query language specifically designed to retrieve data from XML sources. It allows you to navigate through an XML document by defining paths to elements and attributes. With XPath, you can precisely specify which elements to target by identifying parent and child elements, making it possible to extract exactly what you need. With XPath, you have several options for the type of information you can extract. You can retrieve the values of specific elements, the names of attributes and their corresponding values, if the elements contain them, or even the names of the elements themselves. To implement this, craft an XPath expression that navigates directly to the elements or attributes holding the data you need. To extract specific data, such as the title from MARC21 field 245 subfield 'a', you can use an XPath expression to navigate through the MARCXML structure. Here's how to set up and understand this XPath expression:

```
xpath(xml(variables('ResultDNB')), '//[local-name()="datafield" and
@tag="245"]/[local-name()="subfield" and @code="a"]/text()')
```

'xml(variables('ResultDNB'))' transforms the contents of the variable 'ResultDNB' into an XML format that XPath can interpret. This variable contains the raw XML response from the DNB query. The part of the expression '//[local-name()="datafield" and @tag="245"]' targets the field 245$a by taking the 'datafield' with an attribute 'tag' equal to '245'. The forward slash (/) is used to indicate that we're moving from a parent element to one of its child elements. After searching the data field 245, the following '/' tells XPath to look within this 'datafield' element and find a child element that matches the criteria in the next part of the expression. So, '/[local-name()="subfield" and @code="a"]' tells XPath to locate the 'subfield' element (inside 'datafield') with an attribute code="a". Finally, 'text()' extracts the text content of the targeted subfield, ensuring that you only retrieve the actual title text without any surrounding tags.

By using this XPath expression within your workflow, you will be able to capture the publication title directly from the MARCXML data returned by the DNB query. This approach is flexible, allowing you to adjust the XPath expression if you need to access other fields or subfields within the MARC21 format.

To efficiently organise extracted data, you can create a separate 'Compose' action for each field you want to retrieve. It is helpful to rename each Compose action immediately, using a clear and descriptive name that indicates the specific data it is pulling. For example, if you are extracting data from field 245$a in a record from the DNB, you might name this Compose action 'ResultDNB_245A'. This method allows you to manage and track data extraction across multiple fields and sources with clarity. You can repeat this process for as many fields and sources as needed.

The HTTP queries for each source are executed very quickly, so querying multiple sources won't significantly slow down your workflow. The main challenge arises when you need to prioritise which information to keep if different sources provide similar data. Let's say you have data from five external sources (e.g., DNB, BnF, Library of Congress (LOC), KBR and Biblioteca Nacional de España (BNE)) and each of these sources includes a title field. Additionally, you may have a title generated from your AI model, TitlePage.

At this point, you have two options. You could create individual columns in your data table for each field from each source. For example, for field 245$a (title), you would have columns named 'DNB_245A', 'BNF_245A', 'LOC_245A', 'KBR_245A' and 'BNE_245A'. While this approach preserves all extracted data, it can lead to a complex and bulky data structure, especially if you have multiple fields to store for each source. Each field would require its own set of columns, potentially making your table cumbersome to manage.

A more streamlined approach is to define a hierarchy that prioritises which source's data to use when multiple sources provide the same field. For example, you could set up a logic rule for the title field. The logic might specify:

- If 'DNB_245A' is not empty, use this value from DNB for the title
- If 'DNB_245A' is empty, use the value generated by the AI model, TitlePage.

You could further nest conditions for other external sources if both 'DNB_245A' and the AI model's value are empty. This hierarchical system simplifies your data table by keeping only one final value for each field after the logic is applied, rather than maintaining separate columns for each source. Such a conditional structure may appear complex at first, but once it is set up, it will automatically consolidate the most relevant data, leaving you with a clean and prioritised final result for each field.

Add a new row – Dataverse

It is now time to gather all the information and send it to your Dataverse table, where it will be stored. That way it can be visualised in the Power App, modified if necessary and exported when needed. To do this, add the action 'Add a row' (Dataverse). Select your table, 'Book'. When you open the advanced options, you will see all the columns in your table. Next to each field, you can map the corresponding output from previous actions. You can easily use dynamic content to insert this information directly into the fields, but you also have the option to select the tab 'Expression' and use it for replacing characters or other string functions, such as 'lower()' or 'upper()', if any data manipulation is needed. While you could also manually input text directly, this is not required for our specific workflow. For example, in the 'Author1' field, you would insert the value from the 'Extract information from title page' action and continue mapping similarly for the other fields. If you find yourself with more output than expected – for example, when an HTTP query retrieves useful additional information from your sources that you want to import – you can always go back to your table, add a new column and then map the extra data to that newly created field. This process allows you to quickly and easily adjust your workflow as needed, making it flexible and adaptable to handle any extra data or new requirements that may arise.

Some values in your data row can be determined by applying specific conditions. For example, when appending content to the Dataverse field SubjectText, you have two primary sources to consider: (i) the text from the back cover, represented by the variable BackCoverText; and (ii) summaries from external sources, such as the MARC21 field 520$a. Both sources can be stored separately in individual columns or you can combine them by nesting conditions to create a single consolidated value. Deciding how to organise these conditions is a critical step as this preparation directly impacts the subsequent flow for SubjectIndexing. If you want to nest it in the one variable, create a string variable at the start of your flow and name it 'SubjectIndexingText'. This variable will serve as the repository for the text extracted from either the back cover or the external source. Once the variable is established, include an 'Append to string variable' action in your flow. If you have stored the external source data in a compose action named '520$a' (which corresponds to the MARC21 field 520$a from an external source), you can use a formula to dynamically evaluate and assign the appropriate value to SubjectIndexingText. For example, the following formula ensures that the text is selected based on availability:

```
if(equals(empty(outputs('520$a')), true),
if(equals(empty(variables('BackCoverText')), true),
        '',
        variables('BackCoverText')
        ),
        outputs('520$a')
        )
```

This expression is a 'nested if' statement designed to determine a value based on the conditions of outputs('520$a') and the variable BackCoverText. The logic begins with an 'outer if' statement that checks whether outputs('520$a') (the value from the external source) is empty. If it is not empty, the value of outputs('520$a') is directly returned, giving priority to the external summary. However, if outputs('520$a') is empty, the 'nested if' statement is triggered to evaluate the variable BackCoverText. The 'inner if' statement uses the same empty() and equals() logic to check whether BackCoverText contains a value. If BackCoverText is also empty, the expression returns an empty string (''), indicating that neither an external summary nor a back cover text is available. On the other hand, if BackCoverText is not empty, its value is returned.

This structure ensures that the system prioritises the external source when available but seamlessly falls back to the back cover text if the external summary is missing. This flexible approach makes the workflow robust, functioning effectively with or without information from external sources. When using the 'Add a new row' action, you can assign the variable SubjectIndexingText to the relevant field. By doing so, you create an intelligently selected and consolidated text, which is optimised for downstream processes such as subject indexing and entity extraction in the next flow.

Move file to 'Processed' folder

To complete your flow, move the file to the 'Processed' folder, which will also give you a clear visual indication that the process has successfully finished. To do this, use the 'Move file' action, specifying the 'Processed' folder as the destination. By moving the file to this designated folder, you are ensuring that anyone reviewing the process can easily see that the workflow has been fully executed. This step is particularly useful for keeping track of which files have already been handled, avoiding confusion or duplication. This method clearly separates processed files from those still in progress. Incorporating this final action into your flow adds an extra layer of structure and clarity, ensuring that everything runs smoothly from start to finish.

Summary

The first flow 'Analyse' is now completed. This flow is an instant flow, so will start when someone pushes a button in the application. However it is also possible to create an automated cloud flow, which does not require a manual trigger from Power Apps. The process for an automated flow differs slightly from the instant one. To set up an automated cloud flow, begin by using the trigger 'When a file is created (properties only)'. In the trigger settings, select the relevant SharePoint site address and choose the appropriate Document Library (in this case 'Cataloguing') and specify the folder you want the flow to monitor for changes (here, it will be the 'Scans' folder). By configuring these settings, you ensure that the flow is triggered automatically whenever a new file is added to the 'Scans' folder. This automated trigger will initiate the rest of the workflow without needing manual intervention from Power Apps. Once the trigger is in place and activated, the first action you should incorporate into your flow is 'Move file'. This step will handle the movement of files from the 'Scans' folder to a designated folder for processing. The rest is the same as the process outline above. Table 4.2 below gives a summary of the discussed flow and compares the two types of flows: the instant cloud flow and the automated cloud flow.

Table 4.2 *Different flows based on different trigger*

Instant cloud flow	**Automated cloud flow**
Trigger: Start from Power Apps	Trigger: When a file is created (properties only)
Get files (properties only): List all files from a folder in a SharePoint document library	
Apply to each (for each file):	
Move file to Processing Get File Content AI analysis HTTP Searches Subject indexing Entity Extraction Add row to Dataverse Move file to Processed	Move file to Processing Get File Content AI analysis HTTP Searches Subject indexing Entity Extraction Add row to Dataverse Move file to Processed

Both flows ultimately accomplish the same goal, but the choice between them depends on your specific process and needs. One option might suit your workflow better than the other based on how tasks are assigned and carried out. The instant cloud flow is ideal when the person scanning the books is also responsible for validating them. In this scenario, the process is as follows: the individual scans all the books, opens the app, clicks a button within the app that triggers the flow and the records are immediately created, ready for validation. This flow works best when scanning and validation occur in a seamless sequence, handled by the same individual.

If there is a disconnect between the person scanning and the person validating – whether because they are two different people or because these tasks are performed at different times – the automated cloud flow would be more appropriate. This setup allows for a more hands-off approach where the scanning triggers an automatic process, creating records that the validator can access later. This method ensures smoother collaboration and better workflow management when tasks are distributed across team members or timeframes. Choosing the right trigger depends on whether the tasks are centralised with one person or distributed among multiple individuals or periods. By aligning the flow with your specific needs, you can ensure efficiency and ease of use.

Power Automate Flow 'SubjectIndexing'

The 'Analyse' flow is designed to detect metadata and classify it into appropriate fields, ensuring your data is organised effectively. However, to unlock its full potential, you have the option to further enrich your metadata by incorporating advanced processes such as subject indexing and entity extraction. Subject indexing classifies data into categories based on themes or topics. Entity extraction identifies and isolates specific elements within the metadata, such as names, dates or locations, providing a granular understanding of your information. These features offer a significant boost in making your data more actionable, usable and contextually rich.

It is entirely feasible to integrate these processes into the 'Analyse' flow itself, including them after the HTTP searches. However, as workflows grow more complex, modularity becomes crucial. Separating tasks into distinct flows helps maintain clarity and manageability. For this reason, we have opted to describe these steps as part of a different flow. This modular approach keeps your project more organised and allows you to decide whether to include this optional enhancement based on your specific requirements. Although optional, subject indexing and entity extraction can significantly enhance your project by improving searchability and providing richer contextual clarity, empowering users to derive more value from the data. Therefore, we will create a dedicated flow for these steps, one that users can initiate directly from the app by selecting a record. This approach ensures flexibility and user control while streamlining the integration of these powerful tools into your workflow.

Trigger from Power Apps

We will start this flow from within the application, so we need to use the trigger 'Power Apps (V2)', which will initiate the flow from an action within the Power App. Since we will be passing information from the Power App to identify which record or row in the Dataverse table to process, you must create an input for this information in the trigger settings. To do this, add a 'Text' input field. Give this input a meaningful label by renaming 'Input 1' to, for example, 'Identifier'. It is important to leave the field on the right, entitled

'Add your input here', blank. This is because the value for this field will be sent directly from the Power App during the flow.

Initialise a string variable

Start the flow by initialising a string variable, which will serve as the container for the suggested terms, separated by commas. Rename this variable to 'SuggestedSubjectTerms'. Alternatively, you can choose to work with an 'array' if it better suits your requirements. An array is a structured collection of elements, such as strings or numbers, stored together in a single variable. Arrays are particularly useful when working with multiple values that share a common context. In Power Automate, arrays are often used in workflows to handle variable-sized datasets. They are compatible with JavaScript Object Notation (JSON), which is a widely-used format for organising and transferring structured data. JSON arrays allow you to group multiple values into a compact and accessible structure that can be processed by your flow or stored in your database. A sample entry might look like this:

```
["Molecular Biology","Ants","Insect Genetics"]
```

You can also choose for an array of objects where you include additional attributes about each entity. This can look like this:

```
[
{
"term": "Molecular Biology",
"classification": "Science",
"confidenceScore": 0.95
},
{
"term": "Ants",
"classification": "Entomology",
"confidenceScore": 0.97
},
{
"term": "Insect Genetics",
"classification": "Genetics",
"confidenceScore": 0.92
}
]
```

Storing arrays in a database table can be a challenging task as the values are often interpreted as strings rather than actual arrays. This discrepancy can lead to the need for complex operations to manipulate or retrieve the data in its intended format. To simplify this process, at KBR, we have opted to store the values derived from subject terms and extracted entities as a single, comma-separated string. For example, the stored data might appear as Term1,Term2,Term3, representing a collection of terms in a compact format. Later, we will discover how these comma-separated values can be presented to users in a more interactive way in the Power App interface. Instead of a single string, each term will be displayed as an individual checkbox, allowing users to easily select or deselect terms. This setup ensures that users can intuitively decide which terms should be included in the bibliographic record.

Get the correct row

To proceed, retrieve the required data from your Dataverse table by adding the action 'Get a row by ID'. This step is crucial for accessing specific information stored in your Dataverse table. When configuring this action, you must complete two key fields. First, in the Table Name field, specify the name of your Dataverse table – in this scenario, it is named 'Book'. There's no need to modify any settings in the Advanced Options section, so you can leave that area untouched. From this row, we need the value stored in the 'SubjectText' column. As described earlier, this column holds either the back cover text of the book or a summary sourced from external records. This extracted information will play a pivotal role in the subsequent steps of the process.

Translate text

After retrieving the value from the 'SubjectText' column, the next step is to translate the text. This may not be necessary if all your documents are in the same language, but this is rarely the case. Since your category classification model is trained using texts from a specific language, it is crucial that the text sent to the model matches that language. To ensure this, you should add the action 'Translate text into another language'. In this step, select the SubjectText column value, which was retrieved from the Dataverse table, and configure the translation to the language in which your model has been trained. By adding this translation step, you can make sure that text from any language is appropriately converted, allowing your model to perform as intended, regardless of the source language of the documents. In the Advanced Options section you can see that the 'Translate from' is by default set to 'Detect automatically'.

AI model: classify text into categories

After retrieving the value from the 'SubjectText' column, the next step is to use it as input for a custom Category Classification model to automate text classification. To do this, add the action 'Classify text into categories with one of your custom models' to your workflow. In the AI Model field of this action, select one of your published Category Classification models. If you are unsure how to train or publish such a model, refer to Chapter 3, which provides detailed guidance on creating a robust classification model tailored to your specific needs.

The translated text from the previous action acts as the input for this action. This allows the AI model to process the text and generate a comprehensive list of classifications or categories that best describe the content. These categories are based on the patterns and features the model learned during training, ensuring accurate and meaningful classification results. This automated classification saves time and ensures consistency and precision in categorising large volumes of text, enabling efficient data organisation and analysis for your project. The output of this action is structured as an array containing two key values: (i) the classification; and (ii) the confidence score. The confidence score is represented as a floating-point number ranging from 0 to 1, where 1 indicates 100% confidence. For example, a sample confidence score might appear as "score": 0.9979155. This high level of precision helps in assessing the reliability of the classification and ensures accurate data processing for your intended application.

Apply to each classification

Once the classifications are generated by the model, they are processed sequentially. When you add the action 'Append to String Variable' and select the dynamic output 'Classification', Power Automate will automatically create an 'Apply to Each' loop. This loop iterates through the 'Results' array, executing the specified action for each classification entry.

To refine the process, you can set a condition to include only classifications with a confidence score higher than a specific threshold, say 90%. To do this, add a condition to your flow. Move the 'Append to String Variable' action into the 'If Yes' branch of the condition. In the condition setup, choose the dynamic output 'Confidence Score' as the left operand. For the comparison, select 'is greater than' and, in the right operand, enter the value 0.9. This configuration ensures that only classifications with a confidence score above 90% are appended to the string variable. By applying this filter, you maintain a high standard of reliability in the results, ensuring that only the most accurate and relevant terms are included. This approach is particularly useful for tasks requiring high confidence in classification outcomes, allowing your automated process to focus on the most trustworthy predictions. The threshold of 0.9 for the confidence score can be adjusted depending on your specific needs. If you wish to refine the process further to accept only the highest confidence classifications, you can increase this number. Conversely, if you notice that the output tends to be less confident or if the current threshold excludes too many relevant results, you can lower the number to allow a broader range of classifications. This evaluation process is crucial for maintaining the efficiency and accuracy of your app. Over time, as the model's performance is observed in real-world scenarios, you may find it necessary to fine-tune this threshold. Regularly reviewing and adjusting this parameter ensures that your application continues to deliver optimal results and adapts to any changes in the data or classification patterns. For more detailed guidance on maintaining and improving your app's functionality, refer to Chapter 5, which covers best practices for ongoing evaluation and updates.

Update a row in Dataverse

The final step involves updating the original Dataverse record with the generated subject terms. To do this, add the 'Update a row' action in Power Automate. This action ensures that the data you have processed and refined is stored back into the Dataverse table for future use. Identify the specific row to be updated using the RowID from the initial trigger input. This ensures that the correct record, which was processed earlier, is selected for the update.

Next, map the SuggestedSubjectTerms variable to the SubjectTerms column in your Dataverse table. This variable contains the generated and filtered subject terms in a structured format, making it easy to integrate into the record. Once the action is executed, the Dataverse record will be updated with the suggested subject terms. These terms are now readily available for further use, whether for analytics, reporting or integration with other applications. This step completes the workflow and ensures that the enriched data is efficiently stored and accessible for subsequent processes or decision-making tasks.

Summary

By following the above steps, you can build an automated pipeline that categorises text and updates records with meaningful subject terms. In summary, the flow outline is:

- Trigger from Power Apps
  - Text input is RowID
  - This input will be sent from the Power Apps (we will see later that this will be the variable 'varIdentifierRow')
- 'Initialize string variable'
  - Give the name 'SuggestedSubjectTerms'
- Get a row by ID (RowID) – Dataverse
  - Row ID is the text input from the Power App trigger

- Translate text
  - Translate value of column 'SubjectText' into the language from the texts of your AI model
- Classify text into categories with one of your custom models
  - Category Classification model
  - Text = translated text
- Apply to each classification
  - Condition based on confidence score
  - For each classification where confidence score is higher than the installed confidence score, append to string variable: add the classification + comma to the string variable 'SuggestedSubjectTerms'
- Update a row – Dataverse
  - Add the variable 'SuggestSubjectTerms' to the column 'SubjectTerms' of your Dataverse table.

Subject indexing using Annif or GPT

In Chapter 3, we explored other tools, including Annif and a new feature in Power Automate, which allows you to insert GPT-like prompts for analysing text and assigning a (local) classification. These tools offer an alternative approach if you prefer not to use the standard category classification model, providing flexibility in how you handle text categorisation tasks.

If you decide to use Annif, you have the option to set up your own model and API. This involves sending text, either in its original form or translated, via an HTTP POST action to the Annif API. For example, you can begin by testing their pre-trained model using the following base URL: https://api.annif.org/v1/projects/yso-en/suggest. To use this, include the translated text in the request body as follows: text=[outcome of translated text].

This process allows you to evaluate Annif's capabilities with minimal setup before investing in developing your customised model. If you opt to build your own model, it can be tailored to your specific needs, further enhancing its relevance to your data and classification goals.

For those looking to use a local prompt integrated with existing input categories or connected directly to your data source (as detailed in Chapter 3), Power Automate offers another powerful solution. With the action 'Create text with GPT using a prompt', you can specify your desired prompt and link it to the relevant input data. In the 'Input text' box (if your prompt includes an 'input text' variable), you can select the back cover or summary text. The output of this action can be formatted as text or as JSON. The result is a classification tailored to the instructions provided in your prompt, delivering results in the exact format you require. In your prompt, you can specify whether you want a single term or multiple terms , with or without additional context.

Power Automate Flow 'EntityExtractionSummary'

This flow closely resembles the 'SubjectIndexing' flow, so we will primarily focus on highlighting the key differences between the two.

Trigger from Power Apps

This trigger functions in the same way as the one used in the previous flow. It relies on the 'RowID' as the primary text input to get the correct row in the subsequent actions as the RowID serves as a stable and unique identifier.

Initialise a string variable

To begin, initialise a variable or even multiple variables. For better organisation and to keep the flow clear, create a separate variable for each type of entity you want to extract and store. In this example, we will create two variables: 'ExtractedEntitiesCity' and 'ExtractedEntitiesPerson'. These variables will act as containers to hold the extracted entities for each specific type. By creating individual variables for each entity type, you can better manage and track the different entities as they are extracted from the text.

Get the correct row

Begin by identifying the correct row in the dataset and extract the value from SubjectText column as this will serve as the foundation for creating MARC21 6XX fields. The process of deriving this data from a summary is a well-established approach, particularly effective for thematic indexing and subject categorisation. However, it is not the only method available. An alternative strategy involves leveraging entity extraction from the copyright page (a section frequently found in books or documents that provides critical details about authors, editors, illustrators or other key figures involved in the creation of the work). This copyright-page-based method offers a different layer of granularity by focusing on the individuals or groups who directly contributed to the work, thus complementing the thematic focus of summary-based extraction.

To implement this, you need to retrieve the text from the copyright page. This means it has to be integrated in the Power Automate flow 'Analyse', since this flow uses the scan PDF. We outlined how to extract the text from page 4 in order to get the summary, but you can easily apply the same procedure to page 3 to obtain the text from the copyright page. Once this text is captured, entity extraction can be applied specifically to the contributors listed on the copyright page. Copyright-page-based entity extraction can enhance the depth of metadata when incorporated. To adopt this method, you will need to modify the Dataverse table by adding a new column, labelled something like 'Extracted Entities Copyright Page' and create an appropriate variable within the workflow to accommodate this data. Once these adjustments are made, the remainder of the workflow remains unchanged, ensuring a smooth integration of the two approaches.

Detect language of text

When you add the action 'Extract entities from text with the standard model' in the next step, you will notice that the first requirement is to select the language of the text. However, you may not always know the language of the text, which could be a challenge. Fortunately, there is a workaround. You might initially try to use the 'Detect the language being used in text' action, which automatically detects the language of the text. However, this action does not just detect one language; it detects multiple languages within the text. By default, the next step in the flow becomes a For-each loop, where you can process each language detected. While this is useful in some scenarios, we want to avoid triggering the entity extraction process multiple times for each language detected as this could lead to inefficiencies. To address this, follow a similar approach to the previous flow by inserting a 'Translate' action. As the 'Detect from' is set to 'Detect automatically', only the primary language of the text is detected, rather than multiple languages. By focusing on the dominant language, we can streamline the flow and avoid unnecessary duplication of the entity extraction process. In the following step, we can then use the 'Detected language' from the 'Translate' action as the input for the entity extraction action, ensuring that the model processes the text in the correct language without the need for multiple iterations.

AI Model: entity extraction

Now that the language has been detected, you can proceed by adding the 'Extract entities from text with the standard model' action. In the Language field, select 'Custom value' at the end of the list and then choose the 'Detected Language' from the dynamic content that was retrieved in the previous action. For the Text field, do not select the 'Translated text'. Instead, choose the value from the 'SubjectText' field from the Dataverse table. This approach ensures that the entity extraction process uses the original text from the 'SubjectText' column, while still using the correctly detected language for accurate processing. By doing this, you ensure that the entities are extracted based on the primary language of the content. The output from this action will be something like this:

```
{
    "@odata.type": "#Microsoft.Dynamics.CRM.expando",
    "type": "City",
    "startIndex": 10,
    "length": 8,
    "value": "Brussels",
    "score": 0.9
},
```


This extracted information becomes valuable data that you can use in subsequent actions within your flow. As you process the entities, you will obtain key details, such as: the type of entity (e.g., city, person and so on); the startIndex (which indicates where the entity begins within the text); the length (which represents the number of characters the entity spans); the value of the entity (the actual text that matches the entity, e.g., a specific city or person's name); and the score (the confidence score indicating how certain the model is about the entity's accuracy). By capturing these elements, you are able to extract the entities themselves, but you can also gather additional context that can be used for further analysis or conditions. All this data enriches the flow, enabling more advanced and context-aware processing in the following steps.

Apply to each extracted term

Next, add the extracted cities and persons to their respective variables. To do this, set up a condition that checks the type of each entity extracted. Essentially, for each entity, you will check if the type is City; if it is, you'll add the value to the variable ExtractedEntitiesCity. Otherwise, if the entity type is Person, you'll add the value to the ExtractedEntitiesPerson variable. To implement this in Power Automate, add the 'Apply to Each' control and rename it to 'ForEachEntity'. In the 'Apply to Each' control, select 'Entities' as the value to iterate over. Next, add a condition inside the loop to check the type of entity. In the left field of the condition, use the following expression:

```
equals(items('ForEachEntity')?['type'],'City')
```

This checks whether the entity type is 'City'. In the right-hand field, select the expression 'true'. In the 'If Yes' branch of the condition (which will execute if the entity type is 'City'), add an 'Append to string variable' action. Choose the 'ExtractedEntitiesCity' variable and insert the 'entity value' dynamic content, followed by a comma. This will append the city entity to the variable. In the 'If No' branch (which executes if the entity type is not a city), add another condition to check if the entity type is 'Person'. If the condition is true, use the 'Append to string variable' action again, but this time select the

'ExtractedEntitiesPerson' variable and append the 'entity value' + comma for the person. This structure ensures that cities and persons are stored in their respective variables. The use of conditions within the loop ensures that each entity type is handled correctly and efficiently, adding the appropriate value to the right variable for further use in the flow.

Optional: search value in external database

When you identify an extracted entity of the type 'City', you have the option to enrich this data by referencing an external thesaurus, such as GeoNames, to obtain a unique identifier for the city. GeoNames provides a GeoNames ID for cities, which serves as a unique reference, enhancing the utility and accuracy of your data. To integrate this functionality into your workflow, you can set up an HTTP request in Power Automate within the 'If Yes' branch of the condition that checks whether the entity type is a city. To achieve this, include an HTTP action in your workflow. Select 'GET' method and in the URL field, input the following structure:

http://api.geonames.org/searchJSON?q=[Entity Value]& maxRows=1& username=[your_username]

Replace [Entity Value] with the dynamically extracted city name and [your_username] with the username from your GeoNames account. This URL will query GeoNames for the city information, limiting the results to a single entry to ensure precision. The response from GeoNames will be in JSON format, requiring further processing. To handle this, add a 'Parse JSON' action immediately after the HTTP action. Set the Content of the Parse JSON action to the 'Body' output from the HTTP query. For the schema, you can use the 'Generate from sample' option. To generate a sample schema, first run a test to fetch a response from GeoNames. Copy the response body and paste it into the sample generation tool. This step ensures that Power Automate has an accurate understanding of the JSON structure, enabling seamless processing of the GeoNames data. Once the Parse JSON action is configured, you will have access to structured data from the GeoNames response, such as the 'geonameId' field. This unique identifier can be used for further actions in your workflow, such as associating the city with additional metadata or integrating with other systems. By automating this process, you can enhance the accuracy and depth of your data, making your workflow both more efficient and reliable.

Update a row in Dataverse

After completing the preceding steps in your flow, the final task is to include an action to update the relevant data in Dataverse. To do this, add the 'Update a row (Dataverse)' action. This action allows you to modify the data in specific columns with the processed information obtained earlier in the flow. Use the RowID input again to ensure the correct record is updated. Then, map the two variables to the corresponding columns in your Dataverse table. Add the variable ExtractedEntitiesCity in the column Extracted_Entities_Summary_City and the variable ExtractedEntitiesPerson in the column Extracted_Entities_Summary_ Person (as outlined in Table 4.1), assign the city-related data to the first column and the person-related data to the second.

This step ties together all the extracted and processed information, ensuring it is properly stored in a structured format within Dataverse. By updating these columns, you create a clear summary of the entities identified during the flow, making the data more accessible for further analysis in your Power App.

Summary

In summary, this flow successfully extracts all entities from your summary text and stores the entities identified as City and Person into your designated Dataverse table. It automates the process of recognising entities, enriching them as necessary and ensuring they are systematically saved for future use or analysis. The general outline of the flow is structured as follows:

- Trigger from Power Apps
  - Text input is RowID
  - This input will be sent from the Power Apps (we will see later that this will be the variable 'varIdentifierRow')
- 'Initialize string variable'
  - Create two variables 'ExtractedEntitiesCity' and 'ExtractedEntitiesPerson'
- Get a row by ID (RowID) – Dataverse
  - Row ID is the text input from the Power App trigger
- Translate text
  - Translate value of column 'SubjectText', but this action is just to detect the main language of the text
- Extract entities from text with the standard model
  - Standard Entity Extraction model
  - Detected text
- Apply to each classification
  - Condition based on Entity type
    - If City:
      - Optional search in GeoNames

Add entity value to ExtractedEntitiesCity variable
If Person:
Add entity value to ExtractedEntitiesPerson variable
Update a row – Dataverse
Add both variables to their respective associated columns.

Power Automate flow 'CreateRecord' (after validation in the application)

Trigger from Power Apps

The process is similar to the previously mentioned triggers: create a Power Apps (V2) trigger and include a 'RowID' text input to ensure the correct row is retrieved in the subsequent action.

Get the correct row

In this step, use the 'RowID' in the 'Get a row by ID (Dataverse)' action to retrieve the correct row. Unlike the previous flow, where only one specific cell value was needed, this time we require all the columns. This is because we are creating a bibliographic record, which involves consolidating and combining all the extracted, imported and generated information. By pulling in the entire row of data, we can ensure that the bibliographic record is complete and accurate.

Create file content

The next step is to generate the content for the file. To do this, use a 'Compose' action, which allows you to create and structure textual content. In this step, you'll need to decide on the format of the file you want to create. You have the flexibility to generate different types of files, such as MARCXML, BIBFRAME, HTML or any other format that suits your requirements.

The concept is straightforward: once you have your data organised in your table, you can format it however you like. This flexibility allows you to structure the information in a way that best suits your needs. To give you a clear idea of how this works, we will consider a few examples below, focusing specifically on the title and publisher information. Keep in mind that these are just sections of a larger, much more comprehensive record. However, the same formatting principles apply throughout the entire record, ensuring consistency across all parts. By following this approach, you can easily adapt the information to meet specific formatting requirements while keeping the data well-organised and easy to read.

MARCXML:

```
<datafield tag="245" ind1="0" ind2="0">
        <subfield code="a">@{outputs('Get_a_row_by_ID')?['body/title']}</subfield>
        <subfield code="b">@{outputs('Get_a_row_by_ID')?['body/subtitle']}</subfield>
        <subfield code="c">@{outputs('Get_a_row_by_ID')?['body/author1']}
        @{if(
        equals(empty(outputs('Get_a_row_by_ID')?['body/kbr_author2']),true),
        '',
        concat('; ',outputs('Get_a_row_by_ID')?['body/kbr_author2_tp'])
        )
        }
        </subfield>
</datafield>
<datafield tag="264" ind1=" " ind2="1">
        <subfield code="a">@{outputs('Get_a_row_by_ID')?['body/place']}</subfield>
        <subfield code="b">@{outputs('Get_a_row_by_ID')?['body/publisher']}
                </subfield>
        <subfield code="c">@{outputs('Get_a_row_by_ID')?['body/year']}</subfield>
</datafield>
```

In field 245$c, the statement of responsibility, you will notice that it consists of the value from author1, followed by the second part, which is constructed using a conditional expression. This expression works like this: if the value of author2 is empty, nothing is added (''), but if author2 contains a value, a semicolon is inserted, followed by the content of author2. In other words, the system checks whether author2 is populated. If it is, a semicolon neatly separates author1 from author2 to maintain clarity in the field. However, if author2 is blank, the semicolon is omitted to avoid unnecessary punctuation. This approach ensures that the formatting remains clean and accurate, depending on the presence or absence of the second author.

BIBFRAME TURTLE RDF

```
    <http://example.org/instance/1> a bf:Instance ;
    bf:title [
    a bf:Title ;
        bf:titleValue "@{outputs('Get_a_row_by_ID')?['body/title']}" ;
        bf:subtitle "@{outputs('Get_a_row_by_ID')?['body/subtitle']}"
    ] ;
    bf:responsibilityStatement "@{outputs('Get_a_row_by_ID')?['body/author1']}
    @{if(
        equals(empty(outputs('Get_a_row_by_ID')?['body/kbr_author2']),true),
        '',
        concat('; ',outputs('Get_a_row_by_ID')?['body/kbr_author2_tp'])
        )}" ;
    bf:provisionActivity [ a bf:Publication ; bf:date
  "@{outputs('Get_a_row_by_ID')?['body/year']}"^^<http://id.loc.gov/datatypes/edtf> ;
```

```
bflc:simplePlace "@{outputs('Get_a_row_by_ID')?['body/place']}" ;
bflc:simpleAgent "@{outputs('Get_a_row_by_ID')?['body/publisher']}" ;
bflc:simpleDate "@{outputs('Get_a_row_by_ID')?['body/year']}" ; ]
```

SCHEMA.ORG

```
"@context":            "https://schema.org",
"@type":               "Book",
"name":                "@{outputs('Get_a_row_by_ID')?['body/title']}",
"alternativeHeadline": "@{outputs('Get_a_row_by_ID')?['body/subtitle']}"
"author":              {"@type": "Person",
                       "name": "@{outputs('Get_a_row_by_ID')?['body/author1']}"},
"locationCreated":     {"@type": "Place",
                       "name": "@{outputs('Get_a_row_by_ID')?['body/place']}"},
"publisher":           {"@type": "Organisation",
                       "name": "@{outputs('Get_a_row_by_ID')?['body/publisher']}"
"datePublished":       "@{outputs('Get_a_row_by_ID')?['body/year']}"
```

HTML table:

```
<table>
    <tr>
        <td>Title</td>
        <td>@{outputs('Get_a_row_by_ID')?['body/title']}</td>
    </tr>
    <tr>
            <td>Subtitle</td>
            <td>@{outputs('Get_a_row_by_ID')?['body/subtitle']}</td>
    </tr>
    <tr>
        <td>Statement of Responsibility</td>
        <td>@{outputs('Get_a_row_by_ID')?['body/author1']}
            @{if(
            equals(empty(outputs('Get_a_row_by_ID')?
              ['body/kbr_author2']),true),
            '',
            concat(' ; ',outputs('Get_a_row_by_ID')?['body/
            kbr_author2_tp'])
            )}</td>
    </tr>
    <tr>
        <td>Place of publication</td>
        <td>@{outputs('Get_a_row_by_ID')?['body/place']}</td>
    </tr>
    <tr>
        <td>Name of Publisher</td>
        <td>@{outputs('Get_a_row_by_ID')?['body/publisher']}</td>
  </tr>
  <tr>
        <td>Year of Publication</td>
```

```
            <td>@{outputs('Get_a_row_by_ID')?['body/year']}</td>
        </tr>
    </table>
```

All the examples provided above use the raw values of the fields, but of course, before you enter them into Dataverse, there is room for customisation. You can insert additional Compose actions to manipulate specific fields in various ways. For example, you could replace certain values, adjust the capitalisation or even format the data differently to suit your needs. This allows you to clean up or modify the information before it gets sent to your catalogue, ensuring that everything imports exactly how you want. Whether you want to standardise the text, replace outdated terms or simply ensure consistency in formatting, these extra steps offer a flexible way to enhance the quality of your data.

When working with database fields containing multiple values separated by commas, such as columns related to suggested terms or extracted entities, it is essential to implement an 'Apply to each' action to process each individual value. The process begins by splitting the content of the field based on the commas, effectively isolating each value. You can do this using a 'Compose' action with this expression:

```
split([Put here the value of the column],',')
```

This action will split the value of the column based on the separator comma. The output will be a JSON array that can be processed using the Parse JSON action in Power Automate. Once the array is parsed, you can create an action to handle each individual value within it. It is recommended that you append each of these values to a previously initialised variable, formatted in your preferred output structure, such as a MARC21 XML data field. This approach ensures that all values are systematically processed and consolidated into the desired format for further use. By repeating this step for each value, the variable accumulates a collection of MARC21 fields corresponding to the number of entities or terms being processed. After assembling the variable with all the appended fields, you can integrate it into a CreateContent compose action. At this stage, the system dynamically generates the number of MARC21 fields based on the number of values extracted or suggested in the original database field. This method allows for scalable and automated handling of variable-sized datasets. By appending information incrementally to a single variable, you maintain a streamlined and efficient approach to processing multiple entities, ensuring the output aligns seamlessly with the volume of data being handled. This approach simplifies the workflow and maximises flexibility when dealing with dynamic data structures.

We recommend renaming this Compose action to something more descriptive, such as 'CreateContent', and optionally following it with the specific type of output. For example, you could name it as 'CreateContentMARC21' or 'CreateContentBIBFRAME' depending on the format you are working with. This will help keep your workflow organised and make it easier to identify at a glance what each action is doing.

Create and name the file

Once you have created the content for your file, the next step is to generate the actual file. You can create a file on OneDrive or SharePoint or send the files to external servers using API (HTTP Post) or SFTP protocol (Create File-FTP or Create File-SFPT (recommended)).

When deciding on a file name, use a variable to make it dynamic and informative. You could include metadata from your files, such as the title or ISBN if you are working with books. Opt for a variable that is consistently structured but still unique for each file. One simple way to achieve this is by incorporating the date and time of the file's creation down to the second. This ensures that each file name is genuinely unique as it is highly unlikely that two files would be generated at the exact same second. To implement this, click on the field next to 'File name' and insert the following expression:

concat('Import_', formatDateTime(utcNow(), 'yyyyMMddHHmmss'), '.xml')

This will generate a file name like 'Import_20250915110000.xml', assuming the file was created on September 15, 2025, at exactly 11:00:00. This approach ensures each file is uniquely named based on the exact time of creation, making it easy to track and manage multiple files in your system.

When it comes to specifying the file content, insert the outputs of your 'CreateContent' action. To do this, you have two options: (i) select the outputs using the 'Dynamic content' panel, which allows you to easily choose from available actions; or (ii) manually enter the expression in the expression bar. If you opt for the latter, simply type: outputs('CreateContent'). This approach ensures that the content generated by the 'CreateContent' action is accurately transferred to the file, allowing for a seamless and efficient workflow. Whether you are working with MARC21, BIBFRAME or any other format, organising your actions this way will make the process clear and easy to manage. Your flow CreateRecord is now ready.

Create your Power App

To get started with your Power App, navigate to your solution and click on 'New', then select 'App' and choose 'Canvas App'. Right from the beginning, you will need to decide between a tablet/desktop orientation or a phone layout. This choice is crucial because creating a fully responsive Power App that adapts to different screen sizes can be challenging. Therefore, it is important to select the format that best suits your intended use case from the start. Since the app is designed for validating records, the tablet layout is more appropriate as it provides more screen space for working with the data.

Add data and flow

Start by importing the necessary flows into your Power App. To do this, click on the Power Automate icon located on the left side of the screen in Power Apps. Once there, you will see an option to 'Add a flow from this environment'. Go ahead and search for and select the flows you need for your app (Analyse, SubjectIndexing, EntityExtraction and CreateRecord). After importing the flows, the next step is to add the Dataverse table to your app. To do this, click on the data icon on the left side of the screen, which will open the data panel. From here, search for and select the Dataverse table labelled 'Book'. This will establish the connection between your app and the data source. Once these steps are completed, you are all set! With both the flows imported and the Dataverse table connected, your app is now ready for further development and all essential connections are in place for you to start building out its functionality.

Next, it is recommended that you start adding screens to your app. A 'screen' refers to a 'page' within your app and it is essential to carefully plan their structure and layout. Typically, you would start with a home page, which serves as a central hub for navigation. From there, users can move to different sections of the app. However, in some cases, you might want to begin directly with the screen that will be used most frequently to streamline the user experience and minimise unnecessary clicks. For example, if your app involves searching or visualising extracted metadata, you could start with a dedicated 'search screen' as the main interface. This would allow users to immediately access the core functionality they need. You have the flexibility to create as many screens as necessary to support different app features and interactions.

For consistency, it is crucial that all screens maintain a similar look and feel. To achieve this, it is helpful to design a basic, empty screen template that includes key elements like a top header and a navigation menu, but with an empty body section. This template ensures a cohesive visual identity across the app. If you need to add more screens later, you can easily duplicate this basic screen and modify it as needed. Additionally, you may want to create a screen dedicated to holding all your customised buttons. This is particularly useful when building an app that follows your organisation's brand guidelines, such as using specific custom colours, fonts and design elements that reflect your organisation's identity. If you create examples for each of the button elements, with customised background colours, hover effects and font colours based on your organisation's established style, you can easily reuse these components throughout your app. This way, you will not need to manually re-create or modify them from scratch each time you add a new button or element to your app. By saving these customised components, you ensure that every new item adheres to the brand's colour scheme and design principles, rather than defaulting to generic app colours. This approach streamlines the design process and ensures consistency across the app, making the user experience more cohesive and aligned with the organisation's visual identity.

Navigation between screens can be managed using buttons or 'Next' and 'Previous' icons, each configured with an OnSelect parameter. This parameter should include the Navigate([ScreenName]) function, which directs users to the specified screen when the button or icon is selected. The goal is to create an intuitive flow that makes it easy for users to explore different parts of your app without feeling lost or overwhelmed.

To effectively manage the screens in your app, start by clicking on the 'Tree View' icon located on the left side of the screen. This will open up the tree structure, where you can easily organise and navigate through the different parts of your app. Next, click on 'New Screen' to create an additional screen for your app. When you add new screens, it is important to give each one a clear and meaningful name. This will help you understand the purpose of each screen at a glance, making it much easier to maintain and update your app going forward. Clear naming conventions also enhance the overall organisation of your project, particularly as it grows. The app is designed with a straightforward structure that includes three main screens, each with a specific role in the workflow:

1 Search Screen: This allows users to search for and view extracted metadata in an organised manner. When a user selects a record, they are automatically navigated to the Edit Screen, where the Power Automate Flows for Subject Indexing and Entity Extraction are initiated.
2 Edit Screen: Here, users can modify the extracted metadata and manually add any additional metadata as needed. Once edits are complete, the user can press the Validate button to update the record. This action transitions them to the next step below.

3 Validation Screen: Users can finalise the record by selecting specific entities and terms to include. Once selections are made, the final flow CreateRecord is triggered resulting in a comprehensive bibliographic record.

Together, these three screens will form the foundation of your app's core functionality, allowing users to search for records and make modifications with ease. Beyond these primary screens, you might also consider adding additional screens to enhance the app's overall structure and functionality. For example, you could create a Home screen, which serves as a central navigation hub, making it easy for users to jump to different sections of the app or the 'basic empty template' screen or the screen with customised elements for visual consistency. However, for the purposes of this guide, focusing on the three primary screens is sufficient to demonstrate the app's basic functionality. These three screens will provide a clear starting point, allowing users to perform the essential tasks of searching and editing records within the app. Once you are comfortable with these basics, you can expand the app with more screens and features as needed.

SearchScreen – show data using a gallery

Visualise your records

In Power Apps, you can visualise your source data using the Gallery feature. First connect your application with the data. To do this, first select 'Add data source' at the top of the page and then select the Dataverse 'Book' table as the data source. Normally, this data source will be displayed using its plural name, so in our case that would be 'Books'. Once the data are added to the application, go to the SearchScreen, click on 'Insert' and search for Gallery and choose whether you want a vertical or horizontal gallery layout. A vertical gallery displays data in a stacked, vertical list format, while a horizontal gallery arranges the data side by side, in a row. For a cataloguing application, a vertical layout works well as it is often more intuitive and easier to scroll through, especially when browsing extensive lists of items. To implement this, start by adding the gallery component to your screen. However, be mindful not to let the gallery occupy the entire screen. Leave some space at the top of the page for additional elements, such as a search bar (which will be explained in more detail later), navigation icons or action buttons. This reserved space will ensure that users have quick access to essential tools and navigation options without having to scroll or search for them. By organising the layout thoughtfully, you can create a more functional and user-friendly design.

After adding the gallery component to the main section of your screen, the first thing you need to do is link the gallery to the data source containing the information you want to display, in this case, the 'Book' table that you just added to your application. For this example, connect the gallery to the Dataverse table named 'Book'. The 'Items' property will now contain the 'Books' data source. By doing so, the gallery will automatically populate with the data from this table, allowing you to show the book records dynamically.

At this point, it is a good idea to rename the gallery to something meaningful and easy to identify. This helps keep your app organised and makes it easier to refer to the gallery in formulae and other components later. For example, you might choose to name the gallery 'GalleryBooks'.

Next, decide which fields (columns) from your data you want to show for each record. You can choose from several predefined layouts, such as 'Only Title', 'Title and Subtitle', 'Title, Subtitle and Body' or 'Image, Title and Subtitle'. These layouts help you quickly configure how your data is presented. Each field in the predefined layout can then be linked to a column of your table in order to visualise the data. If the predefined options do not fit your needs, you can create a custom layout; for example, you can remove all existing fields and layout. Next, insert a new field by clicking 'Insert' and selecting 'HTML Text'. This allows you to format your data using HTML code for a more personalised presentation.

Let's say you have a Dataverse table with columns named Cover (which contains images), Title, Author and Publisher. To display the cover image, you can select a Gallery layout that includes an 'Image' element or add an Image control manually. In the 'Image' property, type 'ThisItem.Cover' to reference the cover image in your data. Next to the image, you can display other data fields using the 'HTML Text' control. For example, in the HTMLText field, you can type:

<u>"&ThisItem.Title&"</u></br>"&ThisItem.Author&" - "&ThisItem.Publisher

This code will display the title in underlined text, followed by the author's name and the publisher, separated by a dash. This way, you have complete flexibility in styling your data display using HTML. This will be shown like this:

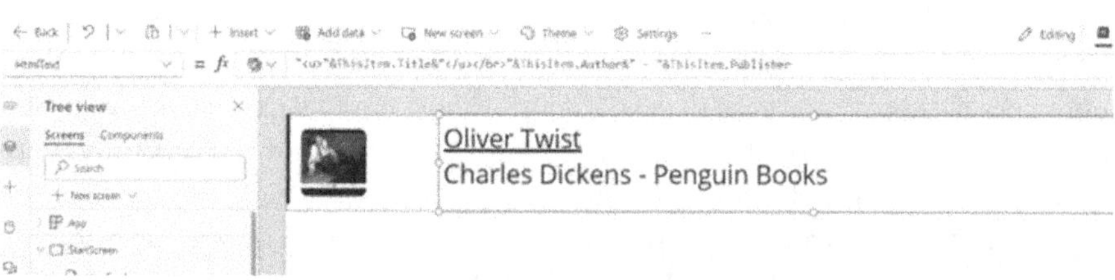

Figure 4.1 *Screenshot of data visualisation in a Power App gallery*

By following these steps, you can effectively visualise and customise your data presentation within the Gallery, making your information both accessible and visually appealing.

Filter and order your records

Adding a search function to your application can greatly enhance its usability, allowing users to quickly find specific items. Implementing this feature is both straightforward and effective. Begin by inserting a TextInput control onto your screen. This will serve as the input field where users can type their search queries. Place it in a prominent location, such as above the gallery, to make it easily accessible. Once the TextInput is in place, you need to configure your gallery to display only the items that match the text entered in the TextInput field. This is achieved by modifying the 'Items' property of the gallery to include a filtering condition. Replace the current value of the gallery's 'Items' property ('Books') with a Filter function. This function will ensure that the gallery dynamically updates to show only the relevant items based on the user's input. The modified formula should look like this:

```
Filter(
Books,
        (IsBlank(TextInput.Text) || TextInput.Text in Title || TextInput.Text in Author)
);
```

'IsBlank(TextInput.Text)' ensures that when the search box is empty, all items in the gallery are displayed. 'TextInput.Text in Title || TextInput.Text in Author' checks if the search text appears in either the 'Title' or the 'Author' fields of the records. Here, the || operator represents the 'or' function, meaning the search will match records where the input is present in either field. You can add other fields that must be indexed in the search.

After setting up the filter, test the feature by entering text into the TextInput field. The gallery should immediately update to show only those records whose 'Title' or 'Author' fields match the input text. If the field is empty, all records should be visible. By following these steps, you create a dynamic search function that improves the user experience by making it easier to locate specific items within the gallery. This method is simple to implement yet provides significant value to the functionality of your app.

You can also customise the order in which records are displayed in your gallery. For example, it may be important to show the most recently created records at the top, ensuring that the latest additions are easily visible. Achieving this is straightforward and involves modifying the 'Items' property of the gallery to include a sorting function. To sort the records, you will use the 'SortByColumns' function. This allows you to specify which column to sort by and whether the sorting should be in ascending or descending order. If your gallery already includes a filter, you can seamlessly combine filtering and sorting within the 'Items' property. For example, if the gallery is filtered based on search input, as explained above, you can add sorting on top of the filter logic. In the following example, the records are sorted based on the 'Created on' column in descending order, so the most recent entries appear at the top. To implement this, update the 'Items' property with the following formula:

```
SortByColumns(
Filter(
Books,
(IsBlank(TextInput.Text) || TextInput.Text in Title || TextInput.Text in Author)
),
"createdon",
SortOrder.Descending
);
```

'SortByColumns(...)' sorts the filtered records based on the 'Created on' column; 'createdon' refers to the column that contains the creation date of each record. Ensure that the column name matches exactly as it appears in your data source. 'SortOrder.Descending' specifies that the sorting should be in descending order, displaying the newest records first. Once the formula is implemented, test the gallery to ensure that it filters the records based on the search input and sorts them correctly, with the latest records appearing at the top.

Displaying records in a specific order, such as most recent first, can be crucial for improving user experience in apps where timely updates or recent entries are important. This combination of filtering and sorting ensures that users can quickly find and interact with the most relevant data.

It is important to know that Power Apps provides helpful suggestions as you start typing the name of a collection, control, action or column of your database in your formula. This feature is designed to make the app development process more efficient and user-friendly. When you begin entering a formula and start typing the name, Power Apps automatically displays a drop-down list of suggestions. When working within a 'SortByColumns' formula, these suggestions also include the names of the columns available in the data source you are referencing. By showing all available elements, Power Apps saves you from needing to remember or manually look up the exact names. This is especially useful in large applications with many different screens, controls and collections. The suggestions help prevent typos or mistakes in column names, ensuring that your formulae are accurate and functional. If you are unsure of the exact name of a column, the drop-down suggestions can serve as a quick reference. That is also why it is important to ensure that your column names in the data source are descriptive and intuitive.

Plan the actions when clicking on a record

Once your gallery is organised, with data clearly and effectively visualised and features like search (filter) functionality and sorting options properly implemented, the final step is to determine what should happen when a user clicks on a specific record in the gallery. This step is crucial as it defines how users interact with the data and what actions are triggered by their input.

When you click on a record, several actions need to take place to ensure a smooth user experience. By default, each record in the gallery will feature an 'arrow right' button located on the right side. This button is typically configured with the action 'Select(Parent)', which is used to select the record itself. However, selecting the record is just the first step. To enable the user to edit the selected record, you must add an additional action. Specifically, you need to configure the 'Navigate' action, which directs the user to the appropriate EditScreen with the edit form in it. This will allow the user to make changes to the selected record.

At this stage, we also need to trigger the SubjectIndexing and EntityExtraction flows. The ideal moment to initiate these is when a record is selected in Power Apps as it allows us to display the results in subsequent fields. Both the SubjectIndexing and EntityExtraction flows require the unique identifier or RowID of the selected record. Since this information is needed multiple times (we will also need it later for the flow 'CreateRecord'), it is more efficient to store it in a variable. This is the right moment to initialise such a variable, ensuring it is set when transitioning to the next screen. But how can you retrieve this identifier effectively? When working with a gallery in Power Apps, you need to identify the record that the user has clicked on. This corresponds to a specific row of data within your data source. From this row, you extract the unique identifier, typically found in a column of your table. By default, this column often shares the table's name. For example, in a table named Book, the unique identifier is likely stored in a column also named Book, containing a distinct combination of numbers or letters that uniquely identifies each record. So, we will need to use that identifier in the variable. Creating a variable can be done using a 'Set' action. You can name the variable whatever you want, but following a consistent naming convention for variables is recommended for clarity. A common practice is to prefix variable names with 'var' for easy identification in suggestions. For example, to store the unique identifier of a selected book record, you can create a variable named 'varRowIdentifier' with the following formula:

Set(varRowIdentifier, GalleryBooks.Selected.Book)

The Set() Function initialises the varRowIdentifier variable with a value. GalleryBooks.Selected.Book retrieves the value of the Book column from the currently selected record in the gallery named GalleryBooks. Once the variable is set, it can be used in subsequent steps, such as other flows. Using variables in this way improves the reusability of your code and enhances maintainability. By following these practices, you can build more efficient, organised and user-friendly Power Apps solutions. Once the variable is set, run the two flows using the SubjectIndexing.Run() and EntityExtraction.Run() actions. In the brackets, you will need to put the input that you need to send to the flows, in this case the varRowIdentifier.

It is important to note that in Power Apps, multiple formulae within a property must be separated by semicolons. To prevent errors and ensure proper functionality, it's a good practice to always include a semicolon at the end of each formula, even if it is not immediately followed by another formula. When all these elements are combined, the complete formula for the 'arrow right' icon in the gallery will look like this:

```
Select(Parent);
Navigate(EditScreen);
Set(varRowIdentifier, GalleryBooks.Selected.Book);
SubjectIndexing.Run(varRowIdentifier);
EntityExtraction.Run(varRowIdentifier);
```

The Select(Parent) function ensures the parent element in a gallery or form is selected. The Navigate(EditScreen) command then moves the user to the EditScreen, where they can modify data. The Set(varRowIdentifier, GalleryBooks.Selected.Book) formula captures the unique identifier of the selected book from the GalleryBooks control and stores it in the variable varRowIdentifier. This variable is then passed as a parameter to the SubjectIndexing.Run and EntityExtraction.Run functions, which initiate workflows for subject indexing and entity extraction. Together, these formulae enable smooth transitions and efficient backend processes as they are executed while you are already navigated to the EditScreen. This ensures that the workflows are complete and ready by the time you reach the third screen, where the results of these flows will be displayed.

EditScreen – edit data using edit form

When you click on a record in a gallery, you are directed to the EditScreen, where you can make changes to the selected record. On this screen, we aim to include a form that allows users to easily edit the record's details and save their modifications. In Power Apps, there are two main types of forms designed for handling data:

1 EditForm: This type of form is specifically used for modifying existing records. It retrieves the selected record's data from the source, displays it in editable fields and allows users to update the information. Once the updates are made, the changes can be saved back to the data source. EditForm is ideal when you want to enable users to make quick updates to an existing item without creating a new one.
2 DisplayForm: This type of form is used to display records in a read-only format. It is particularly useful when you want users to view the details of a record without the risk of making accidental edits. The fields are populated with data from the source but are locked for editing.

By integrating the appropriate form into the EditScreen, you can provide users with a seamless experience tailored to their specific needs, whether it is editing, creating or simply viewing records. If your goal is to enable users to update information about a specific item, using the EditForm is the most appropriate choice. The EditForm is specifically designed for modifying existing records, making it an essential tool for this purpose.

To get started with the EditForm, the first step is to insert the form into your app. Once the form is added, you need to connect it to a data source that contains the records you want to edit, so set the data source of the form again to 'Books'. This connection ensures that the form has access to the data it will display and update. You can always configure the data source by modifying the 'DataSource' property of the EditForm. While the form is now connected to the data source, it does not automatically know which specific record to display for editing. This is where the 'Item' property of the EditForm comes into play. The 'Item' property determines which record from the data source is loaded into the form for editing. To ensure the form shows the correct record, set the 'Item' property to the currently selected record in the gallery from the SearchScreen you are coming from. Since the gallery on your SearchScreen is named 'GalleryBooks', use the following formula in the 'Item' property of the EditForm:

GalleryBooks.Selected

This formula retrieves the record that the user clicked on in the gallery GalleryBooks and shows it in the EditForm. By properly connecting the form to the data source and configuring the 'Item' property, you create a seamless flow where users can select a record from the gallery, navigate to the Edit Screen and update the desired information in a user-friendly manner. The gallery and the edit form and the two screens are now connected. You can enhance navigation by adding icons that allow users to move between screens. Use the 'Navigate' function in the 'OnSelect' property of the icons to achieve this. Here, too, renaming the form to something more distinctive, such as 'EditBookForm', is recommended.

Once you have chosen the record to be displayed in the form, the next step is to configure which fields users can interact with. To do this, use the Properties bar located on the right side of your screen. Under the 'Fields' option, you can add or remove fields as needed. For each field, which corresponds to a column in the underlying table, you have the flexibility to decide whether it will be visible, editable or read-only. This customisation allows you to control both the display and functionality of the form.

By default, a field is displayed using a 'TextInput' control if the related column is configured as a 'Text' data type column. This enables users to view or modify the associated information. However, depending on your requirements, you can replace the default TextInput with other input controls, such as radio buttons, checkboxes or a combo box. These alternative controls are particularly useful when you want to limit the options available to users or provide a more intuitive way to input data. For example, if the underlying column is of the text type but you want to restrict user input to specific values, you can remove the default TextInput and replace it with a checkbox. To ensure the checkbox's state translates correctly into the field's value, you will need to configure the field's 'Update' property in the form. For example, you can use the following formula:

If(Checkbox1.Selected, "Yes", "No")

This formula updates the related column to store the value 'Yes' when the checkbox is selected and 'No' when it is not. Similarly, for a combo box, you can define specific items and use a formula to ensure the selected value maps accurately to the corresponding text field. By customising the input controls and configuring their properties, you can create a user-friendly interface tailored to your application's needs.

Once all your fields have been modified (or corrected) and validated, you need to save the information to update the related table. To achieve this, you can create a 'Submit' button dedicated to saving the information. In the

'OnSelect' property of this button, include a formula that updates the form and saves any changes made to the fields. Since your work on the EditScreen is complete, you can immediately add a Navigate action to transition to the Validation Screen. The formula would look like this:

SubmitForm(EditBookForm);Navigate(ValidationScreen);

Clicking on this button saves your record and opens the last screen.

ValidationScreen

This screen is designed to help users select which entities and suggested subject terms to include in their final record, validate all selections and then proceed to initiate the final CreateRecord flow. It acts as a crucial step in reviewing and customising the data before moving forward.

In the previous screen, the EditForm was introduced as a tool for updating records. However, it is important to note that the EditForm is not the only method available for this purpose. Another option is to use the Patch function, which offers greater flexibility in how data is presented and modified. In this workflow, we will use the Patch function specifically to manage suggested terms and extracted entities.

To make the process user-friendly, it is recommended that you display the automatically generated entities and suggested terms as a list of checkboxes. This intuitive interface allows users to review the system-generated suggestions and decide whether each term or entity should be included in the final record. Users can simply check or uncheck the relevant boxes to make their selections, ensuring full control over the final dataset.

Before implementing this functionality, several preparatory steps are essential to ensure smooth operation. The process begins with the suggested terms stored in a column of the Dataverse table. These terms are saved as a single string, with each value separated by a comma. To work with these terms individually, the data in this column needs to be processed and split into separate values. This step is crucial as it enables each term to be treated as an independent entity, allowing users to review and select them with ease. Once the terms are separated, the next step involves dynamically mapping each value to a checkbox within the user interface for further interaction. The two flows are initiated in SearchScreen by selecting a record. These flows are designed to update the relevant row in the Dataverse table. However, a limitation arises: the updated data from the Dataverse table is not immediately reflected in the application. To address this, it becomes necessary to refresh the data source within the app. After refreshing the data source, the values from specific columns, namely Extracted_Entities_Summary_City,

Extracted_Entities_Summary_Person and Subject_Terms, are stored in variables. Each of these values must then be split into individual terms and separate variables created for each term. This preparation ensures that the terms are readily accessible for further operations or display. The following formula demonstrates the steps required to achieve this functionality, followed by an explanation:

```
Refresh(Books);
Set(varExtractedTerms,Split(GalleryBooks.Selected.Subject_Terms,","));
Set(varTerm1,Index(varExtractedTerms,1));
Set(varTerm2,Index(varExtractedTerms,2));
Set(varTerm3,Index(varExtractedTerms,3));
Set(varTerm4,Index(varExtractedTerms,4));
Set(varTerm5,Index(varExtractedTerms,5));
Set(varExtractedCities,Split(GalleryBooks.Selected.Extracted_Entities_Summary_
        City,","));
Set(varCity1,Index(varExtractedCities,1));
Set(varCity2,Index(varExtractedCities,2));
Set(varCity3,Index(varExtractedCities,3));
Set(varCity4,Index(varExtractedCities,4));
Set(varCity5,Index(varExtractedCities,5));
Set(varExtractedPersons,Split(GalleryBooks.Selected.Extracted_Entities_Summary_
        Persons,","));
Set(varPerson1,Index(varExtractedPersons,1));
Set(varPerson2,Index(varExtractedPersons,2));
Set(varPerson3,Index(varExtractedPersons,3));
Set(varPerson4,Index(varExtractedPersons,4));
Set(varPerson5,Index(varExtractedPersons,5));
```

Here's a detailed breakdown of the formula. The Refresh(Books) function ensures that the most recent data from the Books table in Dataverse is retrieved and available for use in the app. The Set function assigns the split values of Subject_Terms into the variable varExtractedTerms. The Split function separates the string into individual components using a comma as the delimiter. Each term from the varExtractedTerms array is assigned to separate variables (varTerm1, varTerm2, etc.) using the Index function, which retrieves specific values from an array. The columns Extracted_Entities_Summary_City and Extracted_Entities_Summary_Persons undergo the same process, with split values stored in varExtractedCities and varExtractedPersons respectively. These are further divided into individual variables such as varCity1, varCity2 and so forth for cities, and varPerson1, varPerson2, etc., for persons. This structured approach ensures that the terms and entities are processed correctly, providing flexibility for dynamic interface updates and seamless user interaction.

We have not yet discussed where exactly to place this formula. There are two options you can consider. One option is to add the formula to the 'Submit' button of the EditScreen. This way, the formula will execute when you navigate to the ValidationScreen, triggering the process at that specific moment. Alternatively, you could place the formula in the 'OnVisible' property of the SearchScreen. This would ensure that the formula runs whenever the SearchScreen becomes visible. Both approaches have their merits depending on when you want the formula to execute in the flow of your app. The first option is ideal if you want the action tied to the user's submission, while the second option could be useful if you want the formula to run as soon as the SearchScreen is accessed. Consider the flow and user experience you want to create before deciding which approach to use.

Now that you have set all the necessary variables (we have chosen five for each category, but of course, you can create more if needed), the next step is to add the checkboxes to the screen. Set up three columns on the screen: one for terms, one for cities and one for persons. In each column, you will place five checkboxes. For the column containing the terms, adjust the 'Text' property of each checkbox to match the value of the corresponding variable (such as varTerm1.Value, varTerm2.Value and so on). Do the same for the other two categories – cities and persons. By doing this, you will display 15 checkboxes in total, with each checkbox showing the appropriate extracted value for terms, cities or persons. Rename all the checkboxes accordingly (CheckboxTerm1, CheckboxTerm2 ...; CheckboxCity1, CheckboxCity2 ...; CheckboxPerson1, CheckboxPerson2...)

Next, we need to implement a button that will carry out several critical tasks in the system. This button will be designed to update records based on the selections made by the user through checkboxes. Specifically, it will check which checkboxes are marked or unchecked and then reflect those changes accordingly in the system. Additionally, the button will reset any variables that were created during the process, ensuring that the system is reset and prepared for the next operation without any residual data affecting future actions. One of the key actions triggered by this button will be running the CreateRecord flow. This flow is responsible for processing all the updates and ensuring that the changes made through the checkboxes are stored correctly in the database. Once the updates have been processed, the button will also navigate the user back to the SearchScreen, completing the workflow and allowing the user to continue their work seamlessly. In this process, the button will serve as the final step in the workflow. It ensures that all changes are saved, variables are cleared and the user is redirected to the SearchScreen without any interruptions. This smooth transition will make the entire operation more efficient and user-friendly. The formula is structured as follows:

```
Patch(
Books,
EditForm.LastSubmit,
{Subject_Terms: JSON(
[
If(CheckboxTerm1.Value,CheckboxTerm1.Text,""),
If(CheckboxTerm2.Value,CheckboxTerm2.Text,""),
If(CheckboxTerm3.Value,CheckboxTerm3.Text,""),
If(CheckboxTerm4.Value,CheckboxTerm4.Text,""),
If(CheckboxTerm5.Value,CheckboxTerm5.Text,""),
])
}
);
Patch(
Books,
EditForm.LastSubmit,
{Extracted_Entities_Summary_City: JSON(
[
If(CheckboxCity1.Value,CheckboxCity1.Text,""),
If(CheckboxCity2.Value,CheckboxCity2.Text,""),
If(CheckboxCity3.Value,CheckboxCity3.Text,""),
If(CheckboxCity4.Value,CheckboxCity4.Text,""),
If(CheckboxCity5.Value,CheckboxCity5.Text,""),
])
}
);
Patch(
Books,
EditForm.LastSubmit,
{Extracted_Entities_Summary_Person: JSON(
[
If(CheckboxPerson1.Value,CheckboxPerson1.Text,""),
If(CheckboxPerson2.Value,CheckboxPerson2.Text,""),
If(CheckboxPerson3.Value,CheckboxPerson3.Text,""),
If(CheckboxPerson4.Value,CheckboxPerson4.Text,""),
If(CheckboxPerson5.Value,CheckboxPerson5.Text,""),
])
}
);
CreateRecord.Run(varIdentifierRow);
Navigate(SearchScreen);
Set(varCity1, Blank());
Set(varCity2, Blank());
[and do accordingly with the other variables]
```

The formula begins with three Patch functions. These update the Books record based on the checkbox selections for the suggested terms and entities. A Patch function is used to modify or create a record in a data source. The first argument specifies the data source (the Books table) where the update is to be made. The second argument (EditForm.LastSubmit) specifies the record to update. The LastSubmit property refers to the last record successfully submitted by a form control. In this context, the EditForm.LastSubmit property is being used to identify the last record that was submitted via the EditForm on the previous screen. This is important because it allows you to reference and update the exact record in the Books table that was most recently submitted via the form.

The formula checks each of the fifteen checkboxes. From the selected (checked) checkboxes, the text value is added to the record in a (newly created) JSON object (array). If a checkbox is unchecked, its value is ignored. After updating the records, the formula then runs the CreateRecord flow using a variable (varIdentifierRow) that likely identifies the specific record or row that needs to be processed. This ensures that the correct record is handled. This process will generate the final record by merging all relevant information into one comprehensive entry.

It is crucial that this flow is executed only after the Patch functions have been completed. Doing so ensures that all updated information is properly incorporated and handled accurately. If the flow is run before the Patch functions, there's a risk that outdated or incomplete data could be included, leading to inconsistencies or errors in the final record. Sequencing these actions correctly is therefore essential for maintaining the integrity and accuracy of the data. The formula then ensures the user is redirected to the SearchScreen to continue with their workflow. This provides a seamless user experience, bringing users back to where they can perform additional searches or actions.

Lastly, the button resets certain variables (varCity1, varCity2) to blank values, clearing out any data that may have been temporarily stored during the current session. This prevents any unwanted data from interfering with future operations.

Summary of the application

In our application, we implemented an Edit Form that offers users a dual purpose: (i) validating automatically extracted information; and (ii) manually entering additional details about the material. This feature allows users to ensure the accuracy of the bibliographic data while also providing a way to enrich records with custom inputs. For example, users can add specific details such as the number of pages, dimensions and descriptions of the book's contents. Our database is designed to support this hybrid workflow. It includes columns populated with data extracted using AI, such as bibliographic information (e.g., title, author and publication details), which can be reviewed, corrected or updated directly through the Edit Form. Additionally, there are dedicated fields left intentionally blank, allowing cataloguers to input material-specific descriptions. These fields are intended for details that AI can't extract reliably, such as precise measurements, unique features of the book (e.g., illustrations, special bindings) or the presence of specific elements like appendices or indexes. This thoughtful combination of automated data extraction and manual entry ensures that each book in our catalogue has a comprehensive and accurate record. By leveraging AI for efficiency while allowing human expertise to add nuance and context, we can maintain a database that is both detailed and reliable. This application can help streamline the cataloguing process, balancing automation with human input to achieve the best results.

CHAPTER 5

Deploying and Maintaining the Cataloguing Application

To make your application accessible and functional within your organisation, it is essential to follow a few structured steps. These steps will help ensure that the app operates smoothly across different settings, maintains consistent data handling and security and provides the necessary functionality for team members. This chapter provides a detailed guide to setting up the app for organisational use.

Deploying the Power App

Step 1: create separate environments

A critical first step in publishing an application is to establish separate environments for development, testing and production. Each environment serves a unique purpose, allowing you to manage different stages of the app's lifecycle.

Development environment (DEV)

The development environment, often called a 'sandbox', is where initial app creation, experimentation and modifications take place. This space allows developers to freely make changes, test new features and troubleshoot without affecting the live, production version of the app. This separation provides a risk-free environment for trying out new ideas and making adjustments.

It is essential to establish a clear strategy regarding who can make changes and how these changes should be documented. A practical approach might involve designating a small group within your organisation, for example, two or three skilled users familiar with Power Apps, to handle minor changes, such as interface tweaks or simple updates. These should be team members who understand the app and have the knowledge to make adjustments without needing extensive oversight.

For major changes, such as adding complex functionality or rebuilding core features, it might be more efficient to outsource the work to professional Power Platform developers. Collaborating with external experts can be very beneficial, especially for complex updates. However, whenever you work with external partners, maintaining thorough documentation is crucial. This documentation should include an organised overview of the app's structure, detailing key elements such as the app's workflows, Dataverse tables and any automated Power Automate flows. Additionally, it is essential to provide documentation on the security roles within the app, specifying who has access to what data and which actions they can perform. Good documentation helps external developers understand the app's architecture. It also clarifies specific requirements or issues that need addressing. This transparency ensures that all parties involved, internal or external, have a shared understanding of the app's design, functionality and security framework, enabling smoother and more effective collaboration.

Test environment or user acceptance testing (UAT)

A test environment provides a controlled setting where new features and updates can be thoroughly tested before they are deployed to the live production environment. This stage is crucial for ensuring that the app works as intended and functions smoothly with the latest changes. It is particularly valuable for larger teams as it allows developers and end-users to test and validate the newest updates before they are rolled out to the entire organisation.

By using a test environment (that is, an optional environment), users can identify potential bugs, performance issues or usability challenges that might not have been obvious during the development phase. Testing with a more realistic dataset, under conditions that mimic actual user loads, helps ensure that the app will perform well when it reaches a broader audience. This step significantly reduces the risk of disruptions or problems in the live version, giving you a chance to catch and fix issues early. Another key advantage of a test environment is that it allows you to upload and experiment with new data, such as images or other media, to see how the model or specific flows behave in action. Since this environment is separate from the live production environment, any uploads or changes made here will not impact the real production data. This ensures that any issues with the new data, such as errors or unintended consequences, do not affect the actual system or user operations. This safeguard provides peace of mind, knowing that the integrity of your live data is protected during testing and experimentation.

Production environment (PROD)

The production environment is where the live, fully functional version of the app is deployed and made available to end-users within your organisation. This environment serves as the final stage in the app's lifecycle after it has undergone extensive testing and refinement in the development and test environments. Once the app has been thoroughly tested, with any bugs or issues addressed, it is released into production, where it can be used for day-to-day tasks by employees and stakeholders. In the production environment, the app should be stable, reliable and fully optimised for regular use. It is where users interact with the app to perform their routine functions, whether it is accessing data, completing workflows or engaging with other key features. This environment is critical for the app's success as it directly impacts the daily operations of your organisation.

Because the production environment is live, it is essential to ensure that it is monitored and maintained regularly. Any updates or changes made to the app after deployment should be carefully planned and tested in non-production environments first to avoid any disruptions or downtime. Ultimately, a well-maintained production environment allows the app to deliver on its promise of streamlining processes, enhancing collaboration and contributing to the overall success of your organisation.

Step 2: set up security roles

In any organisation, controlling access and defining what users can or can't do within an application is crucial for security and functionality. Security roles are used to specify permissions for different users, based on their roles and responsibilities.

Developer roles

Developers are granted full access to create, edit and delete resources within the development environment. They are responsible for building the application from the ground up, including setting up configurations, managing integrations and pushing updates. This team has control over the development lifecycle, which involves writing and testing code, implementing features, fixing bugs and fine-tuning the app to meet requirements. In addition to managing the app's structure, developers ensure that each update aligns with project objectives and contributes to a stable, functional and secure product.

End-user roles

In the production environment, end-users, such as librarians and cataloguers, interact with the app as part of their regular tasks, supporting activities like organising and accessing information or managing records. These users require permissions to navigate and operate the app effectively but do not need advanced privileges. Limiting their access to only essential functions helps protect the app's underlying configurations and sensitive data elements from unintended modifications.

By tailoring end-user permissions strictly to their daily operational needs, the system maintains a high level of security, enabling end-users to work efficiently without unnecessary complexities or risks. This approach ensures they have access to all the features they need. For any tasks beyond these routine responsibilities, not needed for the daily work, admin roles can be created (see below). This separation of roles creates a streamlined and secure workflow, empowering each user group with precisely the tools they require.

Admin roles

Creating specific roles for administrators can significantly enhance control and monitoring capabilities. Administrators have a broader range of permissions than regular end-users, allowing them to perform functions critical to app management. These roles are designed to handle more advanced functions, providing controlled access to specialised features and management tasks without overloading end-users with options they don't need. For example, they can delete records, an action restricted to admins due to its impact on data integrity. Administrators may also access specialised admin screens that display high-level app performance metrics and settings, giving them insight into the system's operation. Another important function can be the ability to export data, a feature typically unavailable to end-users to prevent unauthorised data sharing. By controlling access to these elevated functions, admin roles help maintain security while supporting application oversight and management.

Assigning the right security roles within each environment is essential for safeguarding an app's settings, data and overall integrity. By carefully managing these roles, you ensure that only authorised users can access critical configurations and sensitive information, minimising the risk of unauthorised changes or data breaches. Security roles can be added or customised directly from the solution interface, making it easy to define access levels that align with each user's responsibilities. Each security role allows you to configure specific permissions, such as creating, reading, updating or deleting data. For example, you might assign a user permission to read and update certain tables without granting them the ability to delete records. This level of control ensures that users have access only to the functions and data necessary for their tasks, enhancing both data security and operational efficiency.

Step 3: export and import the solution

As discussed in Chapter 4, it is essential to organise all app components within a solution. Each environment typically includes configurations such as the application itself, associated flows, databases (like Dataverse), connection references and security roles. By grouping these assets within a solution, as highlighted previously, you create a cohesive package that simplifies management and ensures consistency across environments. Moreover, because solutions can be transferred between environments, placing all components within a solution guarantees that every part of the application – its interface, data, workflows and permissions – moves together, minimising the risk of anything being left behind.

There are two main types of solutions: managed and unmanaged. Unmanaged solutions are ideal for development and testing. They allow flexibility, enabling team members to make changes, experiment and refine the app's components as needed. In this mode, you can adjust tables, flows and other settings without restrictions. Once you are ready to finalise and stabilise the solution for deployment, it can then be exported as a managed solution.

Managed solutions are primarily used for deployment in test (UAT) or production (PROD) environments. When you export a solution as a managed solution, it essentially 'locks' the package, preventing further changes. This safeguard is critical as it ensures the app's integrity by preventing accidental modifications once it has been deployed. A managed solution can be imported into environments without the risk of unauthorised or unintended alterations, providing a reliable and stable version for testing or live use. In summary, organising all application components within a solution makes the management of your app simpler and more efficient, but also enables secure and consistent deployment across environments. The choice between a managed or unmanaged solution depends on the stage of development, with managed solutions offering stability and protection in live environments, while unmanaged solutions allow flexibility during development and testing.

Solutions can be transferred seamlessly from one environment to another, supporting a smooth deployment process as the application moves from development to testing and then to production. In a typical workflow, an unmanaged solution is created and refined in the development (DEV) environment, where flexibility is essential for making and testing changes. Once the solution is stable and ready for release, it is exported as a managed solution. This process is known as the 'deployment procedure'. Deployment is the method by which a completed solution is transferred through different environments. The export–import process of deploying solutions plays a crucial role in maintaining consistency across environments. If new features or improvements are needed, they can be developed in the DEV environment first. Once these changes are validated in the UAT environment, they can be exported and re-imported into the PROD environment. This method of iteratively updating the app helps ensure that the latest features, security enhancements or bug fixes are consistently implemented across all environments.

After deploying the app in the PROD environment, the final step is to share it with users who have the end-user role. This ensures that the intended audience has access to the application and can begin using it as designed. To share the app, navigate to your solution and locate your application. From there, select the 'Share' option, which allows you to manage permissions and specify the individuals or groups with whom the app should be shared. Ensure that the correct users or user groups are added under the 'End-Users' role to avoid unauthorised access or missed permissions.

The application is accessible online, which means you can easily share it with others by copying and sharing its URL. Only people who have been given access to the app will be able to open it. At the top of the app, there is a convenient 'Share' button that provides two options: 'Share' (for copying the URL and sending to other team members who have access) or 'Add to Teams'. By selecting 'Add to Teams', you can integrate the application directly into Microsoft Teams. This integration allows you to access and use the app within the Teams platform itself, creating a unified workspace where users can chat, manage their calendars and work with the app, all in one place. This can be especially beneficial for organisations that rely heavily on Teams as it streamlines workflows by keeping communication, scheduling and the application's functionality accessible in a single, familiar environment. This setup supports a more efficient, seamless work experience for users who prefer to operate within Teams.

By following these steps, you can ensure a smooth rollout of your app within the organisation, with a robust environment structure, clear security permissions and a streamlined deployment process. Each step contributes to a stable and secure application experience, empowering users to leverage the app effectively in their daily workflows.

Maintaining the application

Maintaining and updating a cataloguing app built in Power Platform is essential to ensure its optimal functionality, longevity and security. Effective maintenance involves a combination of proactive measures, regular updates and monitoring to keep the app running smoothly and aligned with user needs. There are several key aspects that a good maintenance plan should include and these are outlined below.

Regularly review and update the flows and application

The flows you have created are not static entities. Once they go live in production, it will not take long before users begin offering suggestions like, 'Wouldn't it be great to include this feature or that functionality?' Be prepared to welcome and act on this feedback. Establish a robust system for collecting user input as this will help you pinpoint pain points and identify desired features. Make it easy for users to share their thoughts, whether through surveys, feedback forms or direct conversations. When feedback starts coming in, take the time to evaluate it carefully. If one user raises a concern or suggests an improvement, check with other users to see if they share the same opinion. This will help you determine whether the proposed change has broader appeal and would add real value. Once you have gathered enough input, assess what is technically feasible. Keep track of these suggestions in a structured way, perhaps as part of a 'wish list' or backlog.

When you have sufficient actionable ideas, translate them into modifications for your flows and the app itself. If you are not the one implementing these changes, compile a detailed 'Requirements Specifications' document to share with potential developers when requesting quotes. Be as specific as possible about the desired changes, ensuring the developers have all the information they need to deliver results that align with your vision.

Additionally, think strategically about how to implement changes. Ask yourself whether it is better to modify an existing flow or create a new, smaller flow to address the need. Keeping flows modular is key to maintaining flexibility and scalability. If a workflow becomes too complex, break it down into smaller, more manageable components. This approach simplifies debugging and updates. It makes future enhancements far easier to implement.

In short, treat your flows and your app as dynamic, evolving tools rather than fixed solutions. By fostering a culture of continuous improvement and ensuring your workflows remain flexible and user-focused, you can build systems that truly meet the needs of your users while staying technically efficient and adaptable over time. This is one of the biggest advantages of the Power Platform environment: the ease with which you can modify existing flows and apps.

Monitor application performance

To ensure your app consistently delivers an optimal user experience, it is crucial to regularly review its performance and monitor key usage and performance metrics. Keep an eye out for inefficiencies, bottlenecks or any issues that could negatively impact the user experience. Identifying these problems early allows for quicker resolution, improving both app performance and user satisfaction. A highly effective way to enhance your monitoring capabilities is by integrating your Power App with Power BI. This integration allows you to create detailed, dynamic visualisations and generate insightful statistics, giving you a clear picture of how your app is performing.

To monitor the confidence levels of AI models effectively, you can set up a workflow that integrates Power Automate, Dataverse and Power BI. Start by adding a new Dataverse table to your solution, such as 'Book Confidence Results', to store the extracted information and confidence levels from your AI model. In your Power Automate flow, include an 'Add a New Row' action for Dataverse after running the model, saving the extracted data alongside the confidence level into this table. Next, connect Power BI to Dataverse by selecting it as the data source and accessing the environments and tables you have permission to use, including the 'Book Confidence Results' table. In Power BI, use visualisation tools to represent key metrics such as the 'Title Confidence Level', showing averages or trends over time for the AI model's 'Title Page' predictions. To ensure your dashboards always display the latest outputs, set up automatic data refreshes and configure a refresh schedule in the Power BI service, particularly for frequently updated data. This seamless integration allows you to analyse AI model outputs in detail, gain actionable insights, monitor performance and drive informed decision making across your organisation.

Test before deployment

Before rolling out updates or modifications to live workflows, it is essential to rigorously test these changes in a dedicated sandbox or the UAT environment. This approach ensures that any potential disruptions to live operations are minimised. While it may seem tempting to deploy small modifications directly to production without thorough testing, try to avoid doing so. Even minor updates can introduce unforeseen errors that disrupt the functionality of the PROD environment. This is particularly critical when multiple individuals rely on the application for their work. A single bug can halt operations, even if only temporarily, creating unnecessary downtime. Even an interruption as brief as an hour can be frustrating for users, impacting their productivity and potentially eroding their trust in the reliability of the application. By investing time in proper testing, you safeguard both the user experience and the reputation of the system, ensuring smoother, more confident transitions when updates go live.

When testing an application, it is a good idea to prepare a set of test files, such as PDFs, that represent various use cases and scenarios within the workflow or application. These examples should be thoughtfully chosen to cover a diverse range of functionalities and potential edge cases. By having a well-prepared 'test set' at hand, you can quickly evaluate the application's features and overall flow. This approach saves time and ensures that all critical aspects of the app are consistently validated. Additionally, using realistic and representative test data helps uncover any subtle issues that might only arise under specific conditions, improving the quality and reliability of the application. In the long run, investing in this systematic testing process contributes to smoother deployments and a more seamless user experience.

Version control

Maintain a detailed version history of the application to effectively track changes and updates. This practice ensures that if an update introduces any issues, you can easily roll back to a previous version, minimising disruptions to users. When working with multiple environments, it is important to recognise that different versions of the application may exist in each environment simultaneously. Typically, the DEV environment will have the most up-to-date version, including the latest changes, features and fixes that have been tested and refined. However, this version may not yet be deployed to the UAT or PROD environments. Therefore, it is essential to keep track of which version of the app is running in each environment to avoid confusion and ensure consistency across the board.

One effective way to manage this is by adding a version number to your application and displaying it on the start screen of the application. This version number acts as a clear indicator of which version of the app users are interacting with, making it easy to differentiate between the latest build and older versions. Whenever you make a major or minor update in the DEV environment, you can update the version number to reflect the new changes. This helps internal teams keep track of which version is being worked on and makes it clear to developers, testers and end-users that the version in the DEV environment is more recent than the one in the UAT or PROD environment. By clearly displaying the version number, you can help streamline communication and prevent any confusion about which features are available in which environments. It also gives users an easy way to verify if they are working with the latest version of the app, improving overall clarity and reducing the chances of errors due to mismatched versions.

Automate maintenance alerts

In a Power Automate flow, it is possible to include a 'send an e-mail' action, providing an automated way to notify users and admin of issues and maintenance. While you can configure the flow to send e-mails in a variety of scenarios, including successful runs, it is generally advisable to reserve e-mail alerts for cases where attention or action is required, such as when an issue arises or a specific task needs to be addressed. For example, if the subject indexing process fails to produce a confident suggestion, an automated e-mail can inform the user that certain books have not been indexed properly. This allows them to manually review and adjust the subject indexing for those books as needed. Similarly, you might set up the workflow to send a detailed e-mail to the administrator containing a list of all instances where an error occurred. This ensures that issues are promptly flagged and can be addressed efficiently.

Additionally, if a flow fails multiple times, the system can automatically notify the flow owner, keeping them informed of recurring problems without requiring constant monitoring. By carefully designing these e-mail triggers, you can ensure that notifications are both meaningful and actionable, enhancing the overall effectiveness of the workflow while minimising unnecessary interruptions.

Documentation and providing training and support

Comprehensive documentation and effective training are vital for empowering users to fully leverage the app's capabilities while reducing reliance on IT support. A well-thought-out approach to these resources ensures users can confidently navigate the app, troubleshoot issues and stay informed about updates, fostering a seamless and productive experience.

Start by creating detailed user manuals or quick-start guides that explain the app's features, outline how to navigate its interface and provide clear instructions for performing common tasks. These guides should be written in simple language and include visual aids such as screenshots to make complex processes easier to understand. To further support users, include a troubleshooting FAQ section addressing common questions or minor issues they may encounter. This proactive measure can help users resolve problems independently, saving time and reducing the need for direct support. It is equally important to ensure the documentation evolves alongside the app; each version should come with an updated guide listing new features or changes, along with detailed explanations of how they enhance functionality or affect existing workflows.

For those who prefer hands-on learning, consider offering optional training workshops. These sessions are particularly useful for onboarding new users or introducing significant updates that may require a deeper understanding of new functionalities. To extend the value of these workshops, record the sessions and make them available as online tutorials or training materials. These resources can serve as a reference for existing users and as a valuable onboarding tool for new team members.

Lastly, establish a clear and accessible support system to address user concerns effectively. This can include providing a dedicated e-mail address, live chat support or a ticketing system to ensure that users can quickly report issues or seek assistance. By combining robust documentation with engaging training and responsive support, you can create an ecosystem where users feel empowered and supported, ultimately maximising the app's impact and value.

Troubleshooting common issues

Despite thorough maintenance, occasional issues may still occur when using Power Automate or in your Power App, making it important to have a systematic approach to troubleshooting.

When encountering failed flows, the first step is to access the Power Automate portal and carefully review the run history for unsuccessful runs. This log provides a detailed breakdown of where the flow encountered errors, allowing you to pinpoint specific actions that need attention. For each failed action, it is essential to examine both the inputs and outputs as these often reveal critical details about the root cause of the problem, such as incorrect data formats, missing variables or unexpected system responses. Additionally, ensure that connectors and permissions are correctly configured. Misconfigured settings, particularly after system updates or changes in user access, can lead to disruptions. Check that all relevant permissions are in place and that the connectors being used have the necessary access to interact with other systems or services involved in the workflow. It is also important to confirm the operational status of dependent services, such as Microsoft Dataverse or external APIs. Outages, updates or incompatibilities in these services can lead to flow failures, so verifying their functionality and ensuring they are up to date is a critical step. In some cases, the issue may stem from actions within the flow that are consuming excessive resources or taking too long to execute. Optimising such actions can significantly improve performance and reduce the likelihood of errors. Similarly, review the workflow to identify unnecessary loops or redundant steps as these can add complexity and strain on system resources.

When addressing problems reported by users, it is often beneficial to begin by analysing the issue directly in the PROD environment. This approach ensures that you are investigating the problem as it occurs in its actual operational context, capturing all relevant data, configurations and real-world variables that might contribute to the issue. By thoroughly examining the PROD environment, you can accurately identify the root cause and determine an appropriate solution. Once the problem has been detected and a solution devised, it is best practice to implement the fix in a controlled manner. Start by fixing the issue in the DEV environment, where you can test and refine it in isolation. This step allows you to verify that the changes resolve the issue without introducing new problems or breaking existing functionality. After validating the solution in the DEV environment, deploy it to the UAT and PROD environments. This systematic approach minimises risk and ensures that the solution is robust, well-tested and ready for real-world application. By following this structured deployment process, you can address user-reported issues efficiently while maintaining the integrity and stability of your systems.

Managing and securing data in Dataverse

Data management is at the heart of maintaining the integrity and efficiency of any cataloguing application. It serves as the backbone for a well-organised, secure and reliable system. Properly defined policies, such as a robust data retention policy, and proactive strategies are vital for effective management. For example, in platforms like Dataverse, a clear framework for deleting records can help streamline operations. Once a catalogue entry is finalised and securely stored in a local catalogue, the corresponding record in Dataverse can be deleted unless it serves a specific purpose such as compliance, backup or historical analysis. To further simplify this process, organisations can define retention periods (e.g., six months to a year) for records that need to remain accessible for auditing or other administrative requirements. Automating these processes (e.g., using Power Automate) ensures consistency while reducing manual effort and errors. Retention policies also need to consider why certain data might need to be preserved. Compliance with legal or regulatory frameworks often mandates retaining specific records for defined periods. Additionally, historical data can provide valuable insights for trend analysis or reporting (using Power BI for example) and operational continuity may require retaining records for ongoing projects or long-term workflows. Recognising these needs helps prioritise and justify data retention strategies.

Backing up data is another cornerstone of good management practices. Regular backups to secure locations can safeguard critical information against accidental loss or technical failures. For managing live data, archiving older records to secondary databases or storage systems can reduce clutter and improve app performance. This approach enhances system responsiveness and supports scalability as data volumes grow.

Finally, securing data is paramount. Role-based access control ensures that sensitive data is only accessible to authorised users, minimising the risk of breaches. Enabling auditing features within platforms like Dataverse allows organisations to track changes and detect any unauthorised modifications, adding a layer of accountability and transparency.

By integrating these strategies, you can create a streamlined, secure and compliant data management framework that supports the cataloguing app's functionality and empowers users with reliable, efficient tools to achieve their goals.

Summary

By embracing consistent maintenance practices, you can ensure that your cataloguing app remains both reliable and fully functional over time. Regular upkeep and diligent data management are essential for preserving the app's longevity and for optimising its performance. These efforts enhance user confidence by creating a stable, efficient platform where tasks can be accomplished smoothly and securely. Moreover, well-maintained software reduces the likelihood of errors, data loss or security vulnerabilities, allowing users to focus on their work without unnecessary interruptions. Ultimately, investing in proper care for your app supports a more productive user experience.

Other cataloguing uses of Power Platform at KBR

The workflow we have outlined is specifically designed for processing books, using AI models to handle the title and copyright pages. However, this approach can be applied to other pages of a book (e.g., table of contents) or a wide range of other handwritten and printed documents. Because of its versatility, the workflow has potential benefits across the entire galleries, libraries, archives and museums (GLAM) sector. These institutions often work with large collections of historical texts and documents, making efficient digitisation essential. The workflow can convert historical handwritten letters to digital text, including entity extraction or sentiment analysis.

Beyond GLAM, this workflow could be a valuable tool for many types of administrative organisations that want to digitise their operations. It offers a seamless way to incorporate paper-based documents into digital systems, enabling smoother, faster and more accurate digital transformation. By automating parts of the text processing with AI, organisations can streamline their document management, reduce manual data entry and improve access to valuable information.

At KBR, we have harnessed the capabilities of Microsoft Power Apps to gather information from diverse sources efficiently. For one particular project, we plan to scan a series of printed library cards and extract all relevant details from each card. Additionally, one department held several boxes filled with handwritten library cards. Since Microsoft's OCR technology is also equipped with (contemporary) handwritten text recognition (HTR), we developed a model to automatically extract information from these handwritten records. For this project, we chose to store the extracted data in an Excel file. This decision was driven by Excel's flexibility in handling data validation and batch processing, which simplified our workflow. Using Excel also streamlined quality control; instead of verifying each entry individually, we could perform broader, batch-level quality checks, making it the ideal tool for overseeing and validating large sets of data in a more efficient way. Information that was kept for years in boxes could now be detected and made accessible in our OPAC. As a side note, people who need to access and review the data generated by the Power App or Flow in Excel do not require a Power App license. This makes it possible to share the output with more team members within the organisation without incurring significant licensing costs. This can be particularly beneficial for departments that rely on the information but do not need to interact with the app.

We are also launching an exciting project focused on early 20th-century printed maps. This collection includes a wealth of historical maps, each containing valuable information that we want to make easily accessible to the public. To achieve this, we have developed and trained an AI model specifically designed to recognise key details on these maps, such as the title, scale, map number, place name and responsible publisher. By implementing this model, we can automate the detection and extraction of all relevant information from each map in the collection. Once this data is extracted, it can be organised and shared in a public database, allowing researchers, historians and enthusiasts easy access to detailed metadata for each map. This will enhance the discoverability of our map collection but also preserve the historical significance of these documents, making them widely accessible for educational and research purposes.

We recently undertook the digitisation of a printed catalogue that documents publishers and printers from Belgium. This catalogue contained detailed information about the publishers, which was organised on structured information sheets. To preserve and enhance the usability of this valuable data, we developed a model inspired by the original layout and format of these information sheets. Using this model, we meticulously extracted all the details and transformed them into a structured CSV file. This digital transformation not only ensures the long-term preservation of the catalogue but also makes the information far more accessible and practical for further use. By converting the data into a digitised format, it can now be easily processed. This project highlights how we were able to quickly adapt our existing application by adding a dedicated module and model specifically tailored to these information sheets. This level of adaptability is one of the greatest strengths of the Power Platform.

Uses of Power Platform within the GLAM sector

In summary, at KBR, we use AI-driven document processing to handle metadata extraction for various types of materials, such as books, library cards and maps. This technology helps us to efficiently sort and categorise information, making these resources more accessible and organised. However, the scope of AI document processing is far broader, with potential applications across many other document types that would benefit greatly from such advanced metadata handling.

Tables of contents within periodicals

Following a presentation of our project at Informatie aan Zee 2023 (Lowagie, 2023c), a congress for Flemish librarians and archivists, we were approached by an educational library interested in enhancing their digital catalogue. They explained that while they currently catalogue only the titles of their periodicals in their OPAC, they want to go further by including individual article titles from each periodical issue. This would allow students researching specific topics to locate relevant articles directly by title, significantly improving access to the content within these periodicals. For this project, we leveraged the AI model's capacity to recognise tables, which proved ideal for processing tables of contents.

To achieve this setup, start by configuring the AI model to recognise tables specifically. In the setup phase, go to the section titled 'Choose Information to Extract' and select 'Table' as the data type. This setting enables the model to treat the table of contents as a cohesive structure, rather than isolating individual titles. After selecting 'Table' as the extraction type, you can specify the individual columns within the table that the model should detect. This step allows you to define exactly which elements in the table of contents need to be captured, such as Article Title, Author, Page Number or any other relevant columns based on the periodical's layout. For each column, identify the data type of the column: this can be Text, Number, Date or Checkbox. For Number and Date, you will need to add a third parameter that specifies what the number or date looks like. Next, in the 'Tag Documents' section, carefully select all the tables of contents you will use for training. For each document, tag the entire table of contents as a structured table. For each table of contents in the training set, tag these specific columns, which will allow the model to understand their layout and position within the table structure.

Once you have selected your table, you can add rows, add columns and add headers. By setting up these rows, columns and headers, you are ensuring that the AI can detect and extract the required data from each table entry in a consistent, organised format. This tagging will help the model differentiate and accurately capture each piece of information within its respective column. This level of detail enables the processed information to be used effectively in your workflow, making it easy to categorise and search for article-specific details in your catalogue. This tagging is crucial as it helps the model understand that it is looking for a table layout, which often varies in structure or in number of rows. By tagging the tables of contents in this way, you are guiding the model to recognise each list as a complete table, rather than as separate, unconnected titles. This structured approach will ensure that, once trained, the AI model accurately identifies and extracts all entries within tables of contents, making it possible to process each article's information efficiently in your automated workflow. Attempting to detect each entry as 'Title1', 'Title2', 'Title3' would be inaccurate and could confuse the AI model during document processing.

Another significant advantage of using table detection is the ability to streamline content processing in Power Automate, making it both efficient and highly adaptable. Once the AI model has detected and extracted the table structure, you can use a 'Compose' action. In Power Automate, when you choose a column from the AI model's output, the system will automatically generate an 'Apply to Each' action. This feature iterates over each row detected within the table, enabling you to define a distinct action for each value or entry. For each row in the table, we can apply specific actions to seamlessly integrate the extracted information into the library's system. One option is to add the data directly to the bibliographic record of the periodical in a MARC21 505 field, which is dedicated to contents notes, allowing each article title to be displayed under the main periodical entry. Alternatively, we can choose to create separate bibliographic records for each individual article title, giving them their own searchable entries within the catalogue. This approach ensures that all relevant article information is systematically organised and indexed, making it easily searchable. As a result, students and researchers looking for specific topics will be able to locate the periodical title and access individual articles directly through the OPAC. This enhancement significantly enriches the library's catalogue, transforming it into a more detailed and user-friendly research tool that empowers users to find precisely what they need more quickly and efficiently.

This is just one example that showcases the incredible potential that the Power Platform offers for adding value to various workflows and processes. By providing more detailed descriptions and clear guidance, it empowers readers to unlock its full capabilities. However, this is only the tip of the iceberg when it comes to what can be achieved with this versatile platform. Countless documents can be efficiently catalogued and indexed using our application.

Personal letters and diaries

Personal letters and official correspondence hold valuable personal and historical information, often revealing a wealth of context about the people, places and events of the time. Other personal documents like diaries offer an intimate, personal lens on historical events, capturing the daily lives, thoughts and emotions of individuals. By applying the Microsoft AI Document processing to these documents, we can extract crucial details, such as names of sender and recipient, date and content of the letter. Additionally, it could be interesting to specifically extract how each letter is opened and closed as these parts often reveal (subtle) details about the relationship between the sender and the recipient. The greeting or salutation might show whether the interaction was formal, friendly or intimate, providing clues about social norms or personal closeness. Similarly, the way a letter is signed off can reflect the level of familiarity, respect or affection in the relationship; these are details that might vary significantly depending on the era, culture or social context. By automatically extracting these elements, they can be analysed to help understand the nuances of historical social dynamics and offer a more layered perspective on interpersonal connections in the past.

The prebuilt Sentiment Analysis model can identify the emotional tone or sentiment behind the text. This allows researchers to gauge levels of optimism, fear, frustration or hope, reflecting the psychological impact of historical events on ordinary people. Through such analysis, letters and diaries become a rich source of data that not only enhances our understanding of the past but also brings history to life through personal stories and perspectives.

Entity Extraction and Category Classification can help to identify the content of the text. Personal names and places mentioned in diaries add context, connecting individuals to specific communities, locations and social networks, which helps researchers trace relationships, social structures and geographic ties.

All these elements can be combined in a Dataverse database in order to facilitate research on a collection of letters. This process enriches our understanding of social networks and historical events and offers insights into the nature of personal relationships from past eras. It can help to map connections between individuals, track changes over time and even piece together the stories of people who may otherwise remain unconnected in traditional records.

Newspapers and periodicals

Newspapers are rich sources of structured data, containing specific elements like headlines, bylines, publication dates, article sections and advertisements. Extracting and organising these components can significantly benefit researchers as it allows for a deeper exploration of historical events, shifts in public opinion and economic trends over time. By extracting headlines, for example, researchers can analyse them and track how major events were reported, how public discourse evolved and how different news sources framed the same issue. Similarly, bylines and dates help build timelines and identify recurring journalists or authors, offering insight into media perspectives and individual reporting styles.

Advertisements in newspapers provide a unique window into the economic landscape of a given period. They reflect consumer behaviour, popular products and prevailing social values. Also, the frequency, style and content of ads can indicate economic cycles, cultural trends and even societal concerns, like health or technology, highlighting how public interests shift over time.

In addition, leveraging image description capabilities to analyse newspaper photographs or illustrations can further enrich historical understanding. AI-driven image recognition can describe the content of these visuals, identifying people, places, objects and scenes. This allows for a fuller picture of the events and social settings represented, complementing the textual information. By describing images, we can capture cultural details, such as fashion trends, architectural styles or even the tone conveyed by a photograph, all of which provide a valuable visual context to the written content.

Indeed, the integration of visual and language processing in newspapers is crucial for fully understanding their complex, multimodal content. Achieving accurate layout parsing is key to enabling AI systems to comprehend the intricate relationships between the various elements, such as stories, photographs, advertisements and headlines, that make up a newspaper page.

While advanced AI techniques, particularly neural network-based deep learning, show great promise in addressing this issue, they still face limitations, especially when it comes to achieving state-of-the-art performance. This remains a significant challenge and it is precisely where we encounter the limitations of document processing models. Each newspaper page can have a unique layout, making it difficult for AI systems to accurately interpret and parse the content. Unlike fixed template documents, where the structure remains consistent across pages, newspapers vary in design, with different arrangements of text, images, advertisements and headlines. This variability poses a major hurdle for document processing models as they must be flexible enough to handle the diverse ways in which information is presented across different editions and publications and even within the same issue. While AI models are improving, the dynamic nature of newspaper layouts means that even the most advanced algorithms may struggle to consistently recognise and organise content. This variability can result in errors, such as misidentifying sections or failing to correctly link related pieces of content, ultimately affecting the model's performance. Thus, while significant progress is being made, fully automating the interpretation of complex, multimodal newspaper pages remains a work in progress, requiring continuous refinement of models and techniques.

One of the primary obstacles is the lack of large-scale, ground-truthed data that is essential for robust and reliable model training. Without a sufficient volume of accurately labelled training data, AI models struggle to achieve the level of accuracy necessary for complex tasks like parsing newspaper layouts. On the other hand, traditional AI methods, such as expert systems that rely on rule-based knowledge encoding, also face difficulties. These systems tend to struggle with generalising across the diverse range of layouts and formats found in different newspapers. This limitation makes them less adaptable to the wide variety of designs and structures that newspapers may adopt, making it difficult to apply one-size-fits-all rules effectively. To address these challenges, innovative visual modelling concepts are being explored. One such approach is probabilistic local text homogeneity (Lu and Dooms, 2021), which holds promise for improving layout comprehension by focusing on the likelihood of textual relationships and spatial arrangements on the page. This approach aims to refine how AI interprets the spatial context in which text and images are arranged, improving its ability to discern logical groupings of content.

Research teams, such as those at the KBR Data Science Lab (where Tan Lu is the in-house researcher), are at the forefront of investigating these and other methods to advance AI's ability to understand the complex layout of newspapers. Their work focuses on integrating visual and textual data in a way that enhances the richness of historical analysis. By pushing the boundaries of AI-driven comprehension, these efforts strive for a more holistic understanding of how newspapers communicate, providing valuable insights for both historical research and digital archiving.

Census records and legal documents

Census documents and other legal documents are invaluable resources for demographic and historical research, providing detailed insights into the population structure, migration patterns and economic conditions of a given period. By extracting specific elements from census records, researchers can piece together a comprehensive picture of individual lives, family structures and broader societal trends. They contain a variety of key data points.

Names allow researchers to identify individuals and trace family lineage, helping build family trees and track population changes across generations. Age data enables researchers to analyse age distribution within a community, identify generational trends and calculate birth years, which are essential for studying life expectancy and age demographics.

Details about the birthplace of parents reveal generational shifts and can highlight migration patterns between generations, showing where populations originated and how communities formed and evolved over time. This data is especially useful in studying the spread of immigrant communities and cultural assimilation over time. For immigrant populations, the year of immigration offers a glimpse into waves of migration and can correlate with historical events, such as economic opportunities, wars or political upheavals that spurred movement.

Address information allows for geographic mapping of communities, showing how neighbourhoods have developed and evolved. It can also reveal socioeconomic status by indicating proximity to industrial centres, educational institutions or wealthier districts. Marriage information, including duration, sheds light on family structure, social norms and marriage trends over time. It also helps track the stability and longevity of relationships in various social or cultural groups. Job details allow researchers to understand the economic composition of a community, highlighting dominant industries, labour trends and gender roles within the workforce. Information on the value of homes and possessions reflects wealth distribution and economic disparities within a population, indicating standards of living and financial stability.

Collectively, these elements offer a comprehensive view of historical communities, shedding light on how populations were structured, how they migrated and how they contributed to the economic and social fabric of their time. Through AI-based extraction and analysis, census data becomes a powerful tool for uncovering hidden stories and trends within our shared history.

Civil registers and church records

Many of the elements found in census documents are also present in civil registers and church records, which are invaluable for genealogical and historical research. Church records, which often include documents like baptismal certificates, marriage registers, burial records and membership lists, contain key details that help trace family lineages, verify life events and offer insights into religious practices and community life. For genealogists, such records are a cornerstone for tracing ancestry as they provide crucial information like names, dates and familial relationships.

Many church records and civil registers share a consistent structure, sometimes consisting of pre-printed templates or standardised forms that were filled in by hand. These pre-printed registers typically have designated spaces for essential information, such as names, dates, places and roles (like parents, witnesses, officiants), which helps maintain uniformity across records from different locations or periods. This structure makes them particularly suitable for the Microsoft Document Processing model as it can read printed (OCR) and handwritten characters (HTR). Using Power Platform, those records can be easily converted into structured digital, searchable formats, allowing for easier access and cross-referencing. For genealogists and historians, this capability significantly reduces the time needed to search through large archives, enabling faster and more comprehensive analysis of family histories, migration trends and social networks. With these structured extraction capabilities, document processing models also facilitate the linking of different records across multiple sources, such as matching a marriage record from a church registry with a baptismal entry or a census document. This interconnectedness allows for a more robust reconstruction of personal and family histories and provides richer insights into the social, religious and demographic patterns of the past.

Photographic archives with captions or annotations

Documents containing images (e.g. photographic archives, postcards, stamps, illustrated brochures, artwork reproductions and even family photo albums) often include captions or annotations with rich metadata. These captions may contain dates, names, locations and even descriptions of events, objects or people captured in the images. Processing and extracting metadata from these captions plays a crucial role in organising and cataloguing visual archives, making it easier for researchers to locate, study and connect visual materials to other historical records. Text recognition, combined with entity extraction, can identify, for example, dates in image captions that provide a chronological anchor. This allows images to be placed within historical timelines, which is essential for understanding the context of significant events or periods. Names, whether of individuals, landmarks, institutions or locations, mentioned in captions help identify subjects and locations, establishing connections between visual artifacts and other records, such as census data, letters and newspapers.

Other types of document

We have discussed some of the most important types of documents where image processing and AI models can be transformative for research, highlighting the immense potential of combining automation with AI. The ability of AI to automate data extraction across varied document types accelerates research and opens up new possibilities for uncovering connections within vast archives. While we can't delve into every document type, here are some additional examples from the GLAM sector where AI-powered processing could be incredibly valuable:

- Travel diaries and ship manifests: These documents record travel routes, passenger lists and cargo. Document processing could extract traveller names, destinations and departure/arrival dates, illuminating migration trends and trade routes.
- Political pamphlets and propaganda: These materials reflect public opinion, political discourse and ideological trends. A model could detect titles, dates, authors, slogans and recurring keywords, providing context for political and social movements.
- Business records (e.g., ledgers, inventories, contracts): These records reveal economic history through sales, expenses and inventories. Models can extract dates, item descriptions, prices and supplier/customer names, helping historians track trade patterns and economic networks.
- School records and yearbooks: These include names, grades, subjects, extracurriculars and occasionally photos. Extracting this data can provide insights into education systems, social networks and youth culture at different points in history.
- Military service records and draft lists: These documents include names, ranks, units, dates of enlistment or service and locations. Extracting these

elements helps in studying military history, the social demographics of the armed forces and the impact of conflicts on communities.
- Guild records and apprenticeship contracts: These documents contain names of craftsmen, apprentices, skills, terms of service and locations. These elements are valuable for understanding labour history, trade skills and the organisation of work in past societies.
- Public announcements: Broadsides and public announcements were used to convey news, laws or events to the public. Detecting headers, dates, issuing authorities and locations helps historians track public events, legal changes and community concerns.
- Medical records: Early medical records include patient names, ailments, treatments and doctors' notes. Extraction of this information is useful for medical history, epidemiological studies and understanding historical healthcare practices.
- Slave registers and abolition documents: These documents record names, ages, origins and transactions related to slavery. Extracting and analysing these details is crucial for tracing genealogy, studying forced migration and exploring the impact of the abolition movement.
- Election ballots and voter registrations: Voter rolls and ballots contain names, addresses, party affiliations and voting outcomes. Processing this data can provide insights into electoral participation, political demographics and shifts in voting patterns.
- Speeches and transcripts of public debates: Transcripts of speeches, parliamentary debates and public forums often have speaker names, dates, topics and positions. Extracting these elements can illuminate the evolution of public opinion, political discourse and legislative history.

Each of these document types contains specific, recurring elements that can reveal historical patterns, trends and societal structures. Processing these documents through extraction models enables the digitisation of data that is otherwise locked in complex or unstructured formats, facilitating accessibility and deeper analysis.

Uses of Power Platform outside the GLAM sector

Here are some examples illustrating how extracting structured information from paper documents can significantly aid various administrative and organisational workflows in transitioning from paper-based to digital formats. This means that the use of these technologies is not only beneficial for handling historical documents and supporting the work of the GLAM sector, but is also incredibly valuable for a wide range of administrative and business applications. By automating the extraction and processing of information, AI-driven tools can streamline operations, reduce manual workloads and improve data accuracy across various sectors. From simplifying document management in corporate settings to enhancing record-keeping in healthcare, education and government, these tools can transform the way information is handled in almost any organisation. This capability extends far beyond preserving history. It holds immense potential for driving efficiency and innovation in today's business and administrative landscapes.

It is important to note that there are already several tools available on the market specifically designed to extract business-related information from bills, invoices and other financial documents and convert that data into digital formats. These tools help businesses automate their invoicing processes, improve accuracy and reduce the need for manual data entry. Of course, platforms like Microsoft Power Platform also offer solutions that can address these needs, providing tools for automation, data processing and integration with other business systems. An important advantage of the Microsoft Power Platform is the adaptability of the models and their ability to integrate seamlessly with existing tools in Microsoft's suite of products. This combination of automation and integration opens up vast possibilities for businesses and administrative workflows. It allows organisations to streamline document processing and improve overall efficiency by ensuring that data flows smoothly between systems. As these AI models continue to evolve, they will offer even more customisation and flexibility, helping businesses better manage their operations, reduce costs and enhance their decision-making processes.

However, when processing personal data, it is essential to consider privacy laws and data protection regulations, especially GDPR in the UK and the EU. Therefore, any data processing involving personal information should be carefully documented, supported by a legal basis or conducted with the informed consent of the individual involved. This ensures compliance and builds trust in the responsible handling of sensitive information.

Most processes today are 'born digital', meaning they are created and stored in a digital environment from the outset. However, not too long ago, administration and record-keeping was done on paper and transforming these paper documents into digital formats can be key to accelerating workflows and improving efficiency. Scanning and extracting data from these paper records allows organisations to create comprehensive digital archives, which are crucial for faster and more efficient processing of information.

For example, hospitals and clinics that once relied on paper records for medical histories, treatment plans and billing can significantly benefit from document processing models. These models can automatically extract key details such as patient names, diagnoses, medications and treatment dates, streamlining access to medical data. This improves the continuity of care but also aids in compliance with health regulations by making records easily accessible and up to date.

Similarly, some tax authorities still process large volumes of paper documents, including tax returns, deductions and financial statements. By using automated document processing, models can extract important information such as income figures, taxpayer IDs and addresses, which speeds up the tax processing cycle. This reduces the risk of human error, supports automated audits and ensures that tax records are processed more efficiently.

Insurance companies, too, deal with vast amounts of paper-based claims and policy documents, which contain valuable information such as client details, claim amounts, incident descriptions and policy terms. By extracting this data digitally, insurance providers can streamline claims processing, identify potential fraud more effectively and manage policies with greater accuracy and speed.

Human resources (HR) departments manage extensive employee records that include employment history, performance reviews, benefits information and more. Automating the processing of these documents allows HR teams to build digital profiles for employees, simplify onboarding, track employee tenure and manage benefits programmes, ultimately improving the overall HR workflow.

In each of these examples, document processing models can greatly increase operational efficiency by reducing manual data entry, improving accuracy and enabling easy access to well-organised digital information. This approach plays a critical role in driving digital transformation across various industries and sectors, enhancing productivity and reducing the administrative burden associated with paper-based workflows. By adopting automation in this way, organisations can streamline their operations and improve the quality and speed of their services.

CHAPTER 6

Conclusion

The book aims to serve as an invaluable guide for anyone looking to develop an application in Power Apps tailored for creating and managing bibliographic records. It provides a hands-on, step-by-step approach to navigating the complexities of this process, making it accessible even to those who may be new to Power Apps or bibliographic systems.

Readers are introduced to a variety of powerful features integral to the application, including advanced metadata detection, which ensures accurate and efficient identification of key bibliographic elements. The book also delves into the use of HTTP queries, enabling seamless interaction with external databases and APIs to fetch or verify information. Additionally, the book explores subject indexing, a critical feature that helps users categorise and organise records effectively, ensuring they are easy to locate and manage. We also cover entity extraction, a sophisticated tool that identifies and isolates meaningful data points from text, streamlining the process of record creation.

Hopefully, now we have reached the conclusion, you will have a comprehensive understanding of how to build a robust and user-friendly application, equipped with features that address the specific needs of bibliographic data management. Whether you're a librarian, an archivist, a developer or a data enthusiast, this resource provides the insights and techniques needed to bring your application to life.

The primary goal of this initiative is to discover and systematically document information that has not yet been catalogued, filling critical gaps in data management. This step is pivotal for creating a more efficient and comprehensive system for handling the ever-expanding volume of information we are presented with. The true value of this process lies in its ability to automate tasks that would otherwise be daunting and time-consuming. By leveraging the latest advancements in technology, this approach drastically minimises the time and effort required to identify and record new information. It serves as a foundation for more nuanced and detailed cataloguing in the future, paving the way for improved data organisation and accessibility. Beyond just efficiency, this method transforms workflows, making it not only possible but practical to tackle cataloguing challenges that once seemed insurmountable due to their labour-intensive nature.

This tool has the potential to revolutionise how institutions manage their collections beyond cataloguing, offering a dual benefit that goes beyond simply addressing cataloguing backlogs. While it is undeniably effective in helping organisations systematically work through existing unprocessed materials, its true power lies in its ability to facilitate deeper, more meaningful indexing of those materials. By converting handwritten and printed text into machine-readable data, where the information is accurately interpreted and placed into the correct fields, this approach transforms information into a resource that is searchable and highly usable and valuable for digital humanities research. By enriching the metadata and creating a more dynamic, interactive way to explore collections, it empowers institutions to bridge the gap between their archives and the communities they serve. This means that collections, often hidden or underutilised, can become vibrant, accessible resources, fostering greater collaboration, learning and discovery. In a world where digital humanities research is growing rapidly, such advancements are not just useful, they are essential for ensuring that historical, cultural and academic materials remain relevant and impactful in the digital age. Researchers, scholars and the broader public can engage with collections in ways that were previously impossible, uncovering connections and insights with greater ease and precision.

This book is not just a guide, it is an invitation. It is an invitation to use this tool but also to become part of something bigger: a community of innovators transforming the way we approach bibliographic cataloguing. By collaborating, we can unlock new possibilities, refine best practices and create solutions that go beyond the needs of today to prepare us for the challenges of tomorrow. With tools like Power Apps and advanced AI features, the potential for innovation is enormous. Whether you are streamlining workflows, enhancing data accuracy or tackling complex cataloguing challenges, these tools empower you to push boundaries and achieve more than you thought possible.

But the value increases even more when we work together. When we share what we have learned, both successes and setbacks, we help each other grow. Likewise, by also sharing training data, we enable others to build their own AI models more easily. Collaboration is essential to revolutionising our field. So, explore, experiment and then share your journey. Together, we can build smarter, more adaptable tools and shape the future of bibliographic cataloguing in ways that truly matter.

References

Billey, A., Nelson, E. and Uhl, R. (2024) *Inclusive Cataloguing: Histories, Context, and Reparative Approaches*, Facet Publishing.

Golub, K., Suominen, O., Mohammed, A. T., Aagaard, H. and Osterman, O. (2024) Automated Dewey Decimal Classification of Swedish Library Metadata Using Annif Software, *Journal of Documentation*, **80** (7), 1057–79, www.emerald.com/insight/content/doi/10.1108/jd-01-2022-0026/full/html.

Harris, J. (2023) *Data Cataloguing: Embracing Artificial Intelligence and Machine Learning for Metadata*, Technics Publications.

Koresi, M. (2024) The Use of AI in the Creation of Metadata in National Libraries. A study submitted in partial fulfilment of the requirements for the MA Library and Information Services Management, University of Sheffield, UK.

Lowagie, H. (2023a) One Automatic Cataloging Flow: Tests and First Results, *IFLA World Library and Information Congress 2023*, https://repository.ifla.org/handle/123456789/2686.

Lowagie, H. (2023b) From Bias to Transparency: Ethical Imperatives in AI-Based Library Cataloging, *IFLA World Library and Information Congress 2023*, https://repository.ifla.org/handle/20.500.14598/2841.

Lowagie, H. (2023c) Het catalogiseren van boeken met behulp van artificiële intelligentie in KBR, *META Tijdschrift voor Bibliotheek en Archief*, **6**, 28–32, www.vvbad.be/meta/meta-nummer-20236/het-catalogiseren-van-boeken-met-behulp-van-artificiele-intelligentie-kbr.

Lu, T. and Dooms, A. (2021) Probabilistic Homogeneity for Document Image Segmentation, *Pattern Recognition*, **109**, https://doi.org/10.1016/j.patcog.2020.107591.

Microsoft, Power Platform Licensing Guide (2024) https://download.microsoft.com/download/9/5/6/9568EFD0-403D-4AE4-95F0-7FACA2CCB2E4/Power%20Platform%20Licensing%20Guide%20February%202024.pdf.

Monyela, M. and Tella, A. (2024) Leveraging Artificial Intelligence for Sustainable Knowledge Organisation in Academic Libraries, *South African Journal of Libraries and Information Science*, **90** (2), https://doi.org/10.7553/90-2-2396.

Nickels, J., Gooding, P. and Terras, M. (2024) The Implications of Handwritten Text Recognition for Accessing the Past as Scale, *Journal of Documentation*, **80** (7), 148–67, https://doi.org/10.1108/jd-09-2023-0183.

Oyighan, D., Ukubeyinje, E. S., David-West, B. T. and Oladokun, B. D. (2024) The Role of AI in Transforming Metadata Management: Insights on Challenges, Opportunities, and Emerging Trends, *Asian Journal of Information Science and Technology*, **14** (2), 20–6, https://doi.org/10.70112/ajist-2024.14.2.4277.

Randtke, W. (2013) Automated Metadata Creation: Possibilities and Pitfalls, *The Serials Librarian*, **64** (1–4), 267–84, https://doi.org/10.1080/0361526X.2013.760286.

Roy, S., Mallikraj, S. V., Moradia, S., Shanta, G., Aravind, S. and Shivaprakash, S. (2024) The Impact of Artificial Intelligence on Cataloging and Classification Systems in Modern Libraries, *Library Progress International*, **44** (3), 769–73.

Salaba, A. and Saccucci, C. (2021) Artificial Intelligence (AI) and Automated Processes for Subject Access, *Cataloguing & Classification Quarterly*, **59** (8), 699–701, www.tandfonline.com/toc/wccq20/59/8.

Stojiljković, S. *Personality Characteristics and Moral Judgement* (1998) Osobine ličnosti i moralno rasuđivanje, *Facta Universitatis*, **5** (1), 507–14, https://scindeks.ceon.rs/article.aspx?artid=0354-46489805507S.

Tait, E. and Pierson, C. M. (2022) Artificial Intelligence and Robots in Libraries: Opportunities in LIS Curriculum for Preparing the Librarians of Tomorrow, *Journal of the Australian Library and Information Association*, **71** (3), 256–74, https://doi.org/10.1080/24750158.2022.2081111.

Tella, A., Odunola, O. A. and Lawal, W. O. (2023) Cataloguing and Classification in the Era of Artificial Intelligence: Benefits and Challenges from the Perspective of Cataloguing Librarians in Oyo State, Nigeria, *Vjesnik Bibliotekara Hrvatske*, **66** (1), https://doi.org/10.30754/vbh.66.1.1031.

Index